THE FUTURE OF MEDICINE

THE FUTURE OF MEDICINE

How We Will Enjoy Longer, Healthier Lives

James Temperton

1 3 5 7 9 10 8 6 4 2

Random House Business
20 Vauxhall Bridge Road
London SW1V 2SA

Random House Business is part of the Penguin Random House
group of companies whose addresses can be found at
global.penguinrandomhouse.com.

Penguin
Random House
UK

First published by Random House Business in 2021
www.penguin.co.uk

A CIP catalogue record for this book is available from the British
Library.

ISBN 9781847943255

Typeset in 9.5/18 pt Exchange Text
by Integra Software Services Pvt. Ltd, Pondicherry

Printed and bound in Great Britain by Clays Ltd, Elcograf S.p.A.

The authorised representative in the EEA is Penguin Random House
Ireland, Morrison Chambers, 32 Nassau Street, Dublin D02 YH68.

Penguin Random House is committed to a sustainable future for
our business, our readers and our planet. This book is made from
Forest Stewardship Council® certified paper.

Contents

Introduction:
The future of you

Which number is greater: the number of galaxies in the observable universe or the number of cells in your body? The answer may surprise you. Our best estimate for the number of cells in the human body is based on an average: a 30-year-old, weighing about 70 kilos, measuring 170 centimetres tall and with a body surface area of 1.85 square metres. This average human is a muddle of variables: their cells vary in size and, depending on where they are in their body, also vary in density. Take these variables into account and tally them up across the average human and you get a very large number: 3.72×10^{13}. Or 37.2 trillion cells.

To work out the number of galaxies in the observable universe you need to point the Hubble Space Telescope at a patch of sky and count up the galaxies. There are caveats: this method doesn't account for galaxies merging over time and misses those we cannot see. But the best estimate we have shows there are between 100 billion and 200 billion galaxies in the observable universe. So 37.2 trillion versus, at most, 200 billion. It's barely even a contest. The number of cells in your body outnumbers galaxies in the universe by 37 trillion. If getting your head around that number is hard, consider this: each trillion is made up of 1,000 billions.

The human body is almost incomprehensibly complex. So it's not surprising that modern medicine should have spent the past 200 years unlocking its mysteries. The first vaccine, for smallpox, was discovered in 1796. Cell theory – the idea that all living organisms are made up of cells – was conceived of in 1839. Back then, life expectancy at birth for men born in England and Wales was 40.2 years. For women it was 42.2 years. Today it stands at 79 years for men and 82.8 years for women. By the end of the century, life expectancy at birth in the world's most developed nations could exceed 100 years. To get there, and beyond, we will enter a new era of healthcare: one where doctors are charged with maintaining health, not treating disease; where one-size-fits-all will be replaced with one-size-fits-one. It's a future where we will all live longer, healthier lives. And this future will be powered by data. Lots of data.

Right now, the majority of healthcare data is based on population averages. That's why, in the UK, all women over the age of 50 are invited for breast-cancer screening every three years. In the US it is recommended that women aged 50–74 get a mammogram every two years. This screening is a best guess, made using data gathered across the population. But what if we knew, from birth, which people had a higher likelihood of developing certain diseases? And what if, throughout our lives, doctors could monitor our bodies based on high-resolution, granular data rather than broad, population-level averages? In the coming decades our medical records won't be a scatter of observations made throughout our lives; instead they will provide a complete picture of who we are, based on data collected about us throughout our lives. This process will begin before birth, when our genomes are sequenced while we are still foetuses. Our genetic records will be carried with us throughout our lives. Over time, our genome will be combined with other biological data, building up a more complete picture of what makes us healthy and what makes us sick. Our personal health profiles will also include data about the individual cells in our bodies and a deep understanding of their function. In combination, these datasets will help doctors make informed and preventative decisions.

You've probably heard of the Human Genome Project – the gold standard for ambitious, groundbreaking science. Completed in 2003, the project successfully sequenced and identified all three billion chemical units that make up our genetic instructions. Adjusted for inflation, the project, which started in 1990, cost $5 billion. You can now get your genome sequenced for less than $200. Genomics has the potential to transform healthcare.

In 2018 researchers in the UK gave us a glimpse of its potential by sequencing the genomes of 100,000 National Health Service (NHS) patients. Participants gave their permission for the data to be linked to information about their medical condition and health records, with that data then being shared with researchers. The aim of the project is to better understand the genetic causes of rare diseases, cancers and infectious diseases. This treasure trove of genetic data has now become a powerful tool for research and diagnosis, with plans to add data from hundreds of thousands more patients over the coming years, to better understand how to treat and prevent disease. And genetic data is just the start. It will be joined by high-resolution data about every facet of our bodies – from wearables that detect the signs of disease before we even display symptoms, to diagnostic tests that hone in on the smallest of irregularities.

This data avalanche has the potential to transform the pharmaceutical industry, informing the creation of treatments that tackle diseases currently seen as either unrealistic targets for drug development or, cruelly, not profitable enough to warrant investment. In many cases the science is ready but the regulators and pharmaceutical companies are not. The clinical trials of today already show what is possible for diseases such as cancer, while research laboratories the world over are focused on the collection and processing of increasingly high-resolution data to uncover the root causes of diseases, both rare and widespread. An aggressive but considered move towards more personalised, precision healthcare will unlock huge benefits. In other cases, egoists and billionaire dreamers imagine an alternate, science-fiction future where all diseases have been cured and death has been solved.

But this isn't a story about ego and hubris. It's a story about heartbreak, sacrifice and survival against all the odds. The story of the future of healthcare is being written by the pioneers of the present; it is the story of how we will all one day come to live, grow old and die. The experts working at the frontier of healthcare all agree that change is necessary and achievable. But they also all agree that change is possible – and soon. In some cases, such as using cell therapy to treat cancer, change is already under way. Regulation is in place and pharmaceutical companies have worked out ways to build profitable, scalable businesses from scientific breakthroughs, with the potential to save many millions of lives. Similar challenges of regulation, scalability and profitably are yet to be realised in fields such as molecular psychiatry and longevity – but that change is coming.

The next wave of technology won't replace the healthcare professionals that exist today, but will rather augment them. A routine trip to the doctor will plug into a vast, potentially global repository of anonymised patient data to help make informed decisions about diagnosis and treatment. Artificial intelligence (AI), already being used at scale by biotechnology start-ups, will become a crucial ally if we are to have any hope of analysing and understanding the exabytes of data collected from billions of patients all across the world.

From genomics to molecular diagnosis and AI-powered drug discovery, the potential of this impending healthcare revolution is immense. But it also comes with challenges. To progress, our society and lawmakers will have to grapple with some of the most challenging questions we have ever faced. If a woman is pregnant and a genetic test shows her child will be born with a debilitating disease, how do we intervene? Removing that genetic mutation would certainly give the child a longer, and arguably happier, life. But determining which conditions are medically 'unacceptable' is fraught with ethical dilemmas. Altering genetics to create so-called 'designer babies' is even more so. Where do you draw the line? In the coming years very many lines will have to be drawn, as we confront issues ranging from the privacy of individual patient data to the ethics of gene modification.

Whatever breakthroughs are achieved, it seems unlikely that they will expand life expectancy to hundreds of years. But it is likely, within your lifetime, that we will be able to provide many billions of people with access to personalised, precision healthcare. By improving healthcare for us all, we can reduce the burden of ill health on our society and our economy. And by doing so, we will all have the opportunity to live longer, happier lives.

CHAPTER ONE
The promise of precision medicine

Mila Makovec loves the great outdoors. Born in November 2010, she grew up on the outskirts of Boulder, Colorado and was skiing by the age of two. Before her third birthday Mila would go on long hikes, preferring to make her own way rather than be carried in a baby backpack. Shortly after her third birthday Mila started rock-climbing. 'This is not just a mom boasting about her child,' says her mother, Julia Vitarello. 'She was really outgoing and advanced. But then,' she adds, 'I started noticing things.' Before she turned four, Mila had started walking with an inturned foot. At the doctor's surgery there was little alarm. Mila was diagnosed with tibial torsion – an inward twisting of the shin bones that is relatively common among toddlers. But, for Julia, the diagnosis didn't add up. Over the coming months Mila became clumsier and clumsier. She would stumble and fall; her speech, previously eloquent and exuberant, became slow and staccato. In 2015, by the time Mila was five, doctors started using the word 'delay' – suggesting that she had been born with something that was hindering her development. 'That didn't make sense,' says Julia. 'Mila was advanced.'

The hunt for a diagnosis was arduous, encompassing more than 100 visits to doctors and therapists. Many doctors who assessed Mila commented on how developmentally advanced she was, despite her ever-growing list of symptoms. Then came the suggestion that maybe, just maybe, she had something incredibly rare. Julia started carrying around a piece of paper to note down any symptoms of a potential neurological condition. 'First it was stepping on toys and breaking them. All the toys in our house were broken. I would ask her, "Mila, what's that in the corner?" and she would say, "Oh, it's a butterfly." The next day I would ask again and she would look away like she didn't know.' Suspecting that Mila might have a vision problem, Julia took her to an ophthalmologist and an optometrist, both of whom said she seemed fine. 'They also told me to chill out,' Julia says.

One day in December 2016 Julia decided she needed some air. She went for a run, got bitten by two dogs and barely flinched. 'I didn't even realise – I'd been crying the whole time for Mila.' Perceiving that she could no longer cope, she packed up a duffel bag, put Mila in the car and drove her to the Emergency Room. 'I heard the word "seizure". I heard the word "blind". She couldn't even stand,' Julia says. Mila spent a week in hospital and received a myriad of tests. 'I saw her decline so quickly. Everything changed that week.' Mila was diagnosed with Batten disease, an incredibly rare genetic disorder that gets progressively worse and is always fatal. 'I felt enormous relief,' says Julia. 'And I also felt very guilty. I'd been told I was crazy for three years, but there it was, in her genetic code.'

Children with Batten disease have a problem with their lysosomes, enzyme-filled bags within cells that clear waste molecules. With defective lysosomes, this waste builds up and kills cells, causing brain damage and, by adolescence, death. Symptoms normally appear between the ages of five and ten years. Children suffer from vision problems and seizures. Their behaviour changes, they become clumsy, their spine starts to curve. The disease is fatal and there is no treatment or cure.

Mila's doctors in Colorado sequenced the protein-coding part of her genome and found an error in one copy of a gene called CLN7, which codes for a protein that it is thought to help molecules move across the membrane of the lysosome bags. To have Batten disease, both copies of CLN7 – one from the mother and one from the father – need to have mutated. Mila's doctors could only find a defective gene from Mila's father. To find the other mutation, Mila's whole genome would need sequencing. At the time few labs in the world – let alone just in the United States – could do this, and even then it was prohibitively expensive and time-consuming. Mila was already six years old and her condition was worsening by the day.

But something else was at stake. Azlan, Mila's younger brother, could also have been carrying the same fatal mutations. If he did, then he would soon start to show the same symptoms. 'I would look at my son, who was totally normal, just like Mila was, and the pain drove me to try and figure out what the mutation was,' Julia says. Without knowing what both mutations were, there was no point checking out her son. To answer that question – and confirm Mila's diagnosis – someone, somewhere, would need to find both mutations.

Faced with such challenges, many parents look to the frontiers of medicine. Julia founded a charity in her daughter's name, Mila's Miracle Foundation, and set herself a fund-raising target of $4 million to put towards scientific research and treatment. Her end-goal was gene therapy. Gains made in this field are slow and expensive, but the need for breakthroughs is acute. Every year 7.9 million children are born worldwide with a serious birth defect of genetic, or partially genetic, origin. That's 6 per cent of all births. An estimated 3.3 million of those children will die before they reach their fifth birthday. Treatments for such diseases are scarce, and cures are almost non-existent. To raise money for research, Julia realised she needed to improve awareness of Batten disease and other similar fatal genetic diseases. 'I learned that my tool was telling Mila's story,' she says. 'So I started telling it to everyone. I let the press into my house, I went on the news. I hated it – I was so sad. But it was the only thing I could do.'

In January 2017 Julia got a phone call from a doctor named Timothy Yu, a neurologist and neurogeneticist at Boston Children's Hospital, whose work just happened to involve sequencing the genomes of people with autism. He had read about Mila on Facebook and wondered if he could help. Yu has run a lab at Boston Children's Hospital since 2000 and has been carrying out whole-genome sequencing since 2010. 'We were one of the first to apply it to human disease,' says Yu. Not only did he think he could help Mila and her family, but the work also aligned perfectly with his academic interests. This gave Yu both the will and, critically, the means to track down the missing mutation. 'My lab has been figuring out how to use high-throughput sequencing to diagnose disease and discover new causes of disease for a long time,' he says. 'We know that there are a lot of cases out there of genetic conditions that go undiagnosed because traditional clinical testing doesn't cut it.'

Yu's task was to find a fragment of a needle hidden in the haystack of Mila's genetic code. The doctors in Colorado had found the mutation from Mila's father, meaning that Yu and his team could focus their efforts on finding the one inherited from Julia. 'At first we struck out,' he recalls. 'All the standard ways of looking at the human genome sequence gave us nothing.' After two days of failure, Yu and his team took a different approach: they started painstakingly combing through the raw genetic data by hand.

The human genome is three billion bases long. To analyse it manually, Yu and his team split it up into chunks that are about 100 letters long and started looking for the one tiny anomaly that would confirm Mila's diagnosis. After days of searching, Yu's team found something. A section within the CLN7 gene inherited from Mila's mother didn't match up properly with the sequence of a normal CLN7 gene. Later analysis would reveal that a 2,000-letter stretch of DNA had 'jumped' and landed there, breaking the gene. This extra chunk of DNA caused an error in Mila's cells, disrupting their ability to make protein. This, in turn, had broken her body's ability to clear out waste molecules. When he called Julia to deliver the news, Yu also had another crucial piece of information to share: while Mila had inherited the mutations from both her mother and father, Azlan had inherited neither. 'That was an enormous, enormous relief,' says Julia. 'But also a huge reminder that Mila was going to die.'

Yu's initial promise to Julia was to find the mutation, and nothing more. But her jumping gene was unusual. It had essentially landed on a part of the gene between the important parts that encode the instructions for making the crucial cell-cleaning protein. Mila's mutation was, it turned out, merely changing the way the instructions were assembled. Most mutations destroy the instructions. In Mila's case, they were disrupted but still intact.

Just as the stars had aligned to connect Mila with Yu, so they aligned again when Yu and his team started to research possible treatments. In December 2016 – only weeks before Yu first spoke to Julia – the Food and Drug Administration (FDA), the US federal agency responsible for drug regulation, had approved a drug called spinraza. The drug is used to treat spinal muscular atrophy, a rare neuromuscular disorder that causes muscle weakness and is a leading genetic cause of death in infants, many of whom die before the age of two. The defect that spinraza targets is the assembly of a critical gene called SMN2. Spinraza reassembles this gene by removing the defect. This type of drug is called an antisense oligonucleotide (ASO) and it works by binding to defective RNA, hiding it and tricking cells into producing a normal protein. Yu had an idea: could he create a similar kind of genetic plaster to cover Mila's fatal defect?

'People were talking about it being curative,' says Yu. 'I went into neurology because there is a huge unmet need. But, in reality, there are very few curative therapies in neurology.' Spinraza changed that. 'When we looked at what spinraza did for those kids and we looked at the mutation that we found in our patient, it was the same story. Why couldn't we pull the same trick?' It was a huge undertaking, made all the more challenging by the fact that Yu and his colleagues had never made a drug before. 'We're an academic lab. I'm a clinician, I'm not a drug developer. But when I looked at the basic science I couldn't see a reason why this wouldn't work.'

Between April and October 2017, Yu and his team created a scientific proof of principle – a new drug, targeted at one tiny mutation in one patient. If it worked, it would become the first single-patient drug ever created. But they faced one additional, potentially insurmountable hurdle: the FDA. 'We weren't looking to commercialise a drug,' says Yu. 'We weren't looking to do what a pharma company would do. What we wanted to do was apply for permission to treat our patient under emergency access.' This regulatory route allows doctors caring for individual patients to, for example, apply to use a drug that has been approved for use on another disease or a drug that is still in development and has not yet gone through clinical trials. If the need is dire – and the application is successful – then the treatment can be used. 'So we decided to choose that path,' says Yu. 'Except that path had never been undertaken for a drug that hadn't undergone some professional development before.' Yu found himself at the frontier of not just medical science, but also regulation. The drug that he and his team had conceived had been developed in an academic lab, not by a pharmaceutical company. Not sure where to start, Yu naively called up an FDA hotline. 'There's a 1–800 number you can call. So I called them up and told them what I wanted to do.' The FDA agreed to set up a conference call, which Yu ended up taking while on holiday. Sitting on the patio of a house that he and his family had rented for the weekend, Yu addressed the

15-member FDA panel. 'It was after this conference call that I realised, "Oh gosh, I think it might be good to get some additional advisers on our side."'

All the while Mila's condition was worsening. One day in the summer of 2017, around six months after the diagnosis, Julia was lying in bed with her daughter. It was dark and Mila, as had become common, was struggling to get her words out. 'Her sentences were getting shorter and shorter. She was saying, "Mommy, Mommy" and she just kept getting stuck on "Mommy". She could never get the rest of the sentence out. She was driving me nuts,' Julia says. 'But then I realised I might never hear her say Mommy again. And that happened. I took a video that night in the dark. And I heard her say "Mommy" and it was just horrible. It was really horrible.' By the autumn of 2017 Mila could no longer speak. All her food had to be blended to the consistency of mashed potato, and even then she choked all the time. She had also been fitted with a gastrostomy tube, in preparation for the day when she would no longer be able to eat or drink.

Back in Boston, Yu and his team were grappling with two challenges: how could they prove their drug was safe to use, and how could they manufacture it quickly enough? To tackle the first challenge, Yu's laboratory tested the drug they had developed on skin and blood samples they had taken from Mila. This process, Yu recalls, was simple enough. But the logistical challenges proved more complex. The drug Yu had created, like spinraza, is known as an antisense oligonucleotide. For a laboratory-grade version of this drug, Yu would expect to pay as little as $10 for a small sample. For a higher quantity, maybe $300. But clinical-grade manufacturing is more costly and complex. Yu started calling around and was told that it would take six to nine months and cost hundreds of thousands of dollars to manufacture a clinical-grade version of his drug. The laboratory-grade version could be turned around in a week. The manufacturers he contacted were also only really geared up to produce huge quantities, perhaps as much as half a kilo. Yu only needed 20–30 grams. Eventually they found a company willing to manufacture the drug in the right quantity and for the right price. The negotiations with the FDA were complex, but, remarkably, Yu continued to make good progress. But time was slipping away and so, in October 2017, manufacturing of the drug began, without FDA approval.

By this point Mila was having up to 30 seizures a day. 'She was smashing her legs and arms against tables. She was bruised. She was going down very quickly,' says Julia. Mila's disease, as is typical for Batten, was manifesting as a series of plateaus and cliffs – for weeks Mila's condition would stabilise, then she would rapidly deteriorate, before stabilising again. Each fall took another chunk of Mila with it. In January 2018, days after Julia and Mila had arrived in Boston hoping that FDA approval was imminent, the good news arrived. 'I was so overwhelmed,' Julia says. Yu assembled his team and asked Julia and Mila to come into Boston Children's Hospital. They were taken to an unremarkable back room, in which sat a refrigerator packed with vials of the new drug. The drug – the first of its kind ever developed for just one patient – now had a name: milasen. Before she received the first dose, Mila's doctors anaesthetised her and carried out one final MRI scan of her brain and spine. Once the scans were done, she was wheeled into the room next door to receive her first dose of milasen, administered via a lumbar puncture.

For Julia and Yu it was the first moment of pause for almost a year. They sat in the MRI waiting room, leaning forward, their elbows on their knees, and they paused. 'I'd been working day and night for the previous year – it was probably one of the most intense professional periods that I'd encountered,' says Yu. 'In the weeks before, people had come up to me saying I was going to lose my licence for this. This is a very risky thing to do. But there was no other help coming. It was very, very clear that if we didn't do anything, she would have no quality of life and she would die within a few short years. I really came to peace with it, professionally and ethically and clinically. So we definitely did pause and take a deep breath and reflect on where we were.'

The day after was blissfully boring. Mila had no adverse reaction to the drug. The first few doses also went without a snag and, over the next six months, Mila's condition started not just to stabilise, but to improve. The number of seizures she had went down drastically and also became less severe. Where before they had been long and violent, now they were short and calm. Mila also began to hold up her own body again and started eating. She even started walking. With her mother standing behind her, their arms interlocked, Mila was able to take a few, stumbling steps. 'It was a pretty big deal,' Julia says.

As the days turned to months, and the months to years, Mila's disease started progressing again – though more slowly than it had before. 'We know it's not all a fairy-tale story,' says Yu. 'We believe this drug is definitely helping, but there are areas in which this disease has progressed that are meaningful and impactful and sad. But I think it has provided her with an improved quality of life.'

Julia agrees. 'Mila has always been a kid who loves imagery and storytelling and songs and has reacted well to nature. I try my best to engage her mind and body.' Most days, a girl the same age as Mila comes round to read her stories. 'If she touches Mila's hands, she feels a child's hands,' Julia says. When Mila's brother Azlan runs around the house and screams and shouts, Mila hears a child's voice. 'I believe, as her mother, that she's absolutely listening and paying attention.'

Mila's story is about so much more than simply one patient. 'It's extremely important to me that all the blood, sweat and tears that we put into milasen is not just for Mila,' says Julia. 'It's opened the eyes of everyone. It's shown what's possible.' The story of Mila represents the most profound realisation of personalised medicine yet. Her legacy, it is hoped, will be to make the path to treatment easier and less expensive for the next patient in desperate need. 'We can imagine a situation where the tools for drug development are good enough, and accessible enough, that a scientist can apply them to a single patient,' says Yu. In this respect, Mila's story is a story from the future. The pharmaceutical industry has already progressed from developing drugs to treat diabetes and heart disease – illnesses that affect millions of people – to develop treatments like spinraza, which target diseases found in only a few thousand patients. Milasen has shown that scientists have the tools at their disposal to develop treatments that can be applied to only one patient with a specific, targetable genetic mutation. 'There's a lot more work to do to be able to prove that the work we did with milasen, as a proof of principle, can be scaled,' Yu says. Now, with an example of how it can work, he believes that healthcare is on the brink of a major change. Antisense oligonucleotides – the genetic plasters behind the success of milasen and spinraza – will likely be the first wave of this change. 'These are incredibly easy to make. You make them out of a machine that's about the size of a large, soft-serve ice-cream machine,' says Yu. 'You type in the sequence, add in the ingredients and the drug is synthesised and comes out twenty-four hours later.' This, says Yu, is a field that can become cheaper and more efficient in a relatively short space of time.

But, as he found while developing milasen, two major hurdles stand in the way: a scientific hurdle and a logistical one. 'I'm a scientist, right? And we've still only done an N of one,' Yu says, using the scientific term for a clinical trial with just one patient. 'If a graduate student comes up to me and shows me an experiment with an N of one, I tell them to go back and do it at least three more times. So conceptually, that's what we need to do.' On the logistical side, Yu realises there are more complex challenges to overcome. 'In order to scale, this process has to be made simpler and less expensive,' he says. More than 70 people were involved in the development of milasen. The cost of the development has never been disclosed, but spinraza, the treatment for spinal muscular atrophy that inspired Yu to develop milasen, costs $750,000 in its first year and $375,000 annually thereafter, placing it among the most expensive drugs in the world.

To be available to the hundreds of thousands of children born with fatal neurodegenerative diseases that can be targeted by antisense oligonucleotides, the price of treatment needs to come down, right down – and fast. For that to happen, drug manufacturers will need to develop processes and business models that enable them to make lots of drugs in very small batches with quick turnaround times. Think going from spending nine months developing one drug to spending one month developing nine drugs. Regulators will also need to introduce new pathways for targeted, small-scale treatments. This will be a huge challenge for an industry that is used to regulating, manufacturing and monetising treatments that can be taken by hundreds of thousands or millions of patients, rather than simply a handful. Or one. Milasen shows that it can be done once, and so Julia and Yu are now focusing their efforts on showing it can be done time and time again.

In the future, the mutations that cause rare, often-fatal diseases could be targeted with precision medicines just like milasen. As whole-genome sequencing costs come down, such checks will become more routine – giving physicians access to all the data they need to make an early and accurate diagnosis. Yu sees a future where parents of children with potentially fatal genetic mutations are immediately connected to experts who can explore the feasibility of making a drug and start the process in days, not months.

Parents could even be screened before they try for a child, to find out if they have mutations that could cause a fatal or life-limiting disease. 'They can know that they have a one-in-four chance of having a child with this disease,' says Yu. The parents would then receive counselling to help them make the best decision. A foetus with an incurable, fatal genetic mutation could be aborted. Or, if *in utero* procedures could correct the genetic fault, treatment could be carried out at the earliest opportunity to give the child the best chance of a long, healthy life. The potential to eradicate some fatal genetic diseases before they even exist is one of the great promises of precision medicine. 'The diagnostic portion is ready to implement right now,' says Yu. 'We just need the political will and the money to do it.'

Julia compares the situation she faced when Mila was diagnosed with Batten to being handed an empty toolbox. Now, that box contains one truly remarkable tool. If – and it's a big if – another child has Batten caused by the exact same genetic mutation as Mila, then there is a fridge in Boston that contains a lifetime's worth of treatment. And if that child is diagnosed sooner than Mila, then there's a chance they could press Pause on the disease and slow its progress earlier – perhaps before that child even displays any symptoms. 'As a clinician and as a human, I think about that all the time,' says Yu. 'What if we could have gotten to Mila sooner? What if we'd been able to make this diagnosis in Mila at age four? We only met her at age six.' Batten is a disease that gains momentum – cells in the brain start dying, symptoms compile and accelerate. 'Coupling this kind of approach with earlier diagnosis is just so critical,' says Yu.

'No one wants to hear the story of a dying child,' says Julia. 'But when it's told in the light of hope, people want to listen.'

CHAPTER TWO

The future of diagnosis

'Medicine is broken,' says Michael Snyder, chair of the genetics department at Stanford University. And Snyder is out to fix it, for each and every one of us. 'We wait until people get ill – and it's really expensive,' he says. Think about it: you go and see your doctor when your body does something it shouldn't. Take Type 2 diabetes as an example. In many people, the disease remains undiagnosed for years. And it's only when symptoms start to build up – regular trips to the bathroom, lethargy, weight loss, blurred vision – that people consult a doctor. Globally, as of 2015, it is estimated that 392 million people have Type 2 diabetes. The disease is treatable, but is also associated with a 10-year shorter life expectancy. The best approach? See the disease coming and stop it in its tracks.

From rare diseases to conditions that affect millions of people, Snyder believes a radically different approach to healthcare is needed.

'Our big shtick is trying to understand what it means to be healthy, and use advanced technologies to keep people healthy,' says Snyder. Consider your last trip to the doctor: the appointment probably lasted fewer than 15 minutes, during which time you had your temperature taken, your blood pressure read and your pulse checked. 'A lot of those measurements are worthless or crude,' says Snyder. And so, in 2009, he embarked on the most detailed study of a single human being in the history of science. The subject of the experiment? Snyder himself.

At the start of the experiment, Snyder's genome was sequenced. Then his colleagues took samples of his blood, urine, nasal microbiome and gut microbiome. He dubbed the process 'personal omics profiling' or, jokingly, the Snyderome – named after the myriad of -omes that make us who we are: our genome, epigenome, transcriptome, proteome, metabolome, autoantibody-ome and microbiome.

But the big data grab wasn't a one-off. The same measurements were taken once every two to three months while Snyder was healthy, and even more regularly when he got sick. This enabled him to understand not only how his body behaved when everything was normal, but also the changes that occurred when he was unwell – and to track those changes over time. Straight away Snyder's omics profile revealed something significant: his genome showed that he was at risk for Type 2 diabetes. Over the next 14 months, Snyder and his team analysed his blood, tracking 40,000 molecules. In 2011 Snyder got a nasty viral infection, which, the data revealed, pushed him over the line to become diabetic. His big data experiment had yielded a remarkable result. 'I remember going to my physician and she says, "What are you doing here? You don't look like you're diabetic – you don't have family history." But the data was correct, and tests carried out by Snyder's doctor confirmed his diagnosis: he had Type 2 diabetes. In response, Snyder changed his diet and started exercising more to bring his diabetes under control.

By 2014 Snyder's omics data revealed that he was diabetic again. Further analysis showed the specific reason: he wasn't releasing insulin from his pancreas. This revelation enabled his doctor to prescribe him a specific drug, called repaglinide, which encourages the pancreas to produce insulin. Snyder's blood-glucose levels went down right away. Repaglinide is far from an obvious treatment – in fact, it's likely that Snyder's doctor might have considered it only after trying three or four other drugs, potentially delaying effective treatment by years. Snyder is still diabetic, but by taking the right drugs he is able to keep the disease under control – and he's still recording billions of data points from his body, in a bid to make further discoveries. 'This is precision diabetes. It's the essence of precision health,' he says.

Shortly after Snyder and his team started recording his own omics profile, they recruited 108 additional volunteers for a far larger version of the trial. These recruits – along with Snyder – received a turbocharged version of a healthcare system that could one day become commonplace. First, their genomes were sequenced. Then, every three months, they gave blood, stool, urine and cheek swab samples. Some wore glucose monitors, others heartbeat trackers. 'We got so much backlash when we started this,' says Snyder. 'People thought that sequencing the genome of healthy people was wrong. A lot of people still feel that way – that we're going to make everyone hypochondriacs. Well, it turns out the average person has, at most, three actionable variants. And these are things that can change people's lives.' This focus on actionable data is key to the success of personalised healthcare. With so much data available, medical experts have to be able to draw the correct conclusions and act on them effectively – no mean feat, when you're drowning in data.

In 2019 Snyder and his team published their results and detailed 67 major health discoveries in the volunteer group. Eighteen people had stage-two hypertension. One had diabetes, a diagnosis that had been missed for years during conventional check-ups. Another volunteer had a genetic variant that is linked to weakened heart muscles. A scan revealed that their heart was defective, and they are now on medication to control the condition. Another volunteer who suffered from regular strokes had a genetic mutation that made the medication they were on ineffective. Doctors were able to act on all of these discoveries, with patients either being told to change their lifestyles or take medication to control their conditions. These interventions weren't only made more precise as a result of omics data, they were also made earlier.

But perhaps the most significant finding from the study was how different people came to suffer from the same disease. 'There are tons of diabetics running around,' says Snyder. 'But how are they getting diabetic?' In his study, nine volunteers developed diabetes. Two became diabetic due to weight gain, and another two, like Snyder, had a sudden spike in glucose levels and became diabetic. The other five volunteers gradually became diabetic without gaining weight. 'No matter what ome we look at, everybody is different,' he says. To understand why, Snyder and his team gathered together data from 12 of their volunteers to map their cytokines, metabolome, transcriptome and clinical lab results over time. When displayed on a scatter chart – with each point representing a different sample, and each colour a different patient – the individuality of Snyder's volunteers becomes clear. On the charts all the light-blue data points, which represent Snyder himself, are bunched together. The same goes for all the red, yellow, blue and purple data points. Each volunteer is an individual – a cluster of coloured dots forming distinct islands of data points. 'This is why medicine is broken,' says Snyder. 'Every decision about your health is based on population-based measurements. But everybody's baseline is different. Making a recommendation for you based on other people's data doesn't make any sense.'

There's an experiment you can do at home to show how true this is. The average oral temperature for an adult human is 37°C. But some people run hot and other people run cold. A healthy baseline for one person might, for example, be 34.7°C. A normal temperature for someone else might be 37.2°C. 'In today's world, if you go to a physician's office and your baseline is normally 34.7°C, then they'll measure you at 37°C and tell you everything is fine and tell you to go home. But if you're up by that much, I guarantee that you're not healthy. And you'd never know it.'

The solution to this broken model, says Snyder, is a dizzying quantity of data. Within the next two decades he believes that genome sequencing before birth will become commonplace. At birth, hundreds (if not thousands) of data points will be recorded and analysed. Then, rather than treating individuals based on a one-size-fits-all model, doctors will be able to treat patients based on their individual data. Each of us will have an omics profile – a detailed, longitudinal view of our health, built up throughout our lives. And this omics profile will give each and every one of us a baseline against which our future health can be assessed. Data recorded in a clinical setting – samples of our blood, urine, stool, saliva and gut microbiome – will be combined with yet more data gathered by wearables and smart devices. By doing this, the doctors of the future will identify diseases, and treat them, before symptoms appear. Take diabetes, for example. It is estimated that 415 million people are currently living with the disease – and 46 per cent of them are undiagnosed. Spotting the early warning signs of diabetes using omics data could bring that number right down. In 2019 alone, it's estimated that the direct cost of treating diabetes worldwide was $760 billion. And that's just diabetes. Early intervention isn't only good for people's health, it's also good for the economy.

As well as data gathered from samples taken by a doctor, data gathered by wearables also plays a crucial role in Snyder's vision of personalised medicine. Right now, the average smartwatch takes more than 250,000 measurements a day. Across the industry there are almost 1,000 different devices, from smart scales and sleep trackers to connected pulse oximeters and electronic personal dosimeters that can track, among other things, movement, heart rate, skin temperature, blood-oxygen levels, sleep, weight and blood pressure. For most people, almost all of these measurements will be superfluous. To accurately track our health, Snyder says, most of us will rely on the fitness trackers and smartwatches that are already ubiquitous – from Fitbit to Garmin and the Apple Watch. And the revolution here will be in where the data they collect ends up.

These devices might collect an increasingly impressive variety of measurements, but they don't do it particularly accurately. 'Some of these measurements are a little off,' says Snyder. 'But it doesn't matter – it's the delta that counts.' By delta, Snyder means change. While wearables aren't great at accuracy, they are good at measuring changes from your normal baseline. That's important because it enables consumer-grade wearables to gather clinically useful data. As part of his own omics profiling, Snyder spent years wearing a myriad of wearables and sensors, with the data streamed in real-time to his phone. This, combined with clinical data, helped him understand just how useful wearables can be.

In 2015 Snyder was on a flight from the US to Norway for a family holiday. He knew, from previous flights, that his oxygen levels dipped while in the air and that his heart rate increased around take-off – both these readings, it turned out, are fairly typical when people fly. But this time Snyder's levels didn't return to normal when he landed. Something was up. Snyder racked his brains for a cause. Two weeks earlier he had been helping his brother build a fence in rural Massachusetts, a known hotspot for ticks infected with Lyme disease. Back in Norway, a blood test confirmed that his immune system was reacting to something, but, unfamiliar with Lyme disease, a local doctor said he should take penicillin. Snyder insisted that the doctor prescribe him doxycycline, a standard antibiotic treatment for Lyme disease. Before he was even sick, the sensors on Snyder's body had picked up that he was unwell. This, in turn, enabled him to make an early diagnosis and receive the correct treatment. Back in

America, Snyder took a blood test for Lyme disease. The results were positive, confirming that he had indeed been bitten by a tick in Massachusetts.

This use of longitudinal data from wearables could, in theory, have far more widespread applications. Snyder and his team are among several groups looking at whether wearable fitness trackers could provide an early warning of a Covid-19 infection. The project involves training algorithms to spot changes in heart-rate data and blood-oxygen levels, both of which can be tracked by consumer wearables. 'You're following people's baselines,' says Snyder. 'And we can pick up when people are ill, before they realise it.' In early trials Snyder and his team were able to pick up the disease before symptoms were displayed in one-third of people. In another third, the disease was picked up by the algorithm at the same time as symptoms were displayed; and in the final third the algorithm only spotted the disease after symptoms appeared. The system is device agnostic – a Fitbit is just as good as a Garmin or an Apple Watch; all the device needs to be able to do is measure your heart rate frequently and detect abnormalities. Snyder's hope is that the technology will soon be able to send out push-notifications to smartphones telling people they may have Covid-19 – potentially helping to slow the spread of the disease.

Fitbit, which was purchased by Google in 2019 for $2.1 billion, is conducting similar trials of its own. Oura, a sensor-packed finger ring produced by Oura Health, is being used by the National Basketball League to track the heart rates and temperatures of players and staff; and the PGA Tour is using a similar wristband developed by Whoop, a Boston-based start-up, to track players, caddies and media during golf tournaments. It's a crucial early stress test of a key component of Snyder's vision for precision medicine. 'This is a big deal,' he says.

Caveats abound. Even if Snyder's Covid-19 algorithm is accurate in detecting a Covid-19 infection before symptoms appear, the data received from wearables might be misleading. The algorithm could, for example, mistake another illness for Covid-19. Then there's contextual data that the algorithm can't possibly know about. 'Maybe you're watching a scary movie,' Snyder jokes. 'Maybe you're under stress. The alarm will go off, but you have to contextualise it.' Such challenges are inevitable as people learn both to live with increasingly detailed, on-demand health data and to interpret accurately what the data is telling them and act accordingly.

As in so many areas of healthcare, Covid-19 is causing rapid change in the field of precision medicine. Seven years ago, when Snyder started his research into the use of consumer wearables, the market for such devices was huge, but most people weren't using the devices to their potential. 'Wearables were just being used as fitness trackers,' he says. 'People figured out how many steps they ran, occasionally looked at their heart rate and then three months later threw them in a drawer.' Now 21 per cent of Americans regularly wear a fitness-tracking watch or wristband – with half of that number supporting the sharing of their data with health researchers. If, through their research into Covid-19, Snyder and his colleagues at other institutions can convince the public that these unassuming scraps of metal and plastic are essential health accessories, then that number could jump considerably.

Snyder's work on Covid-19 is made possible not only by the proliferation of wearable devices, but also by huge advances in our ability to process and understand the data they collect. Two of the world's biggest technology companies have already made strides here: Apple launched HealthKit, a software-development kit for healthcare applications, in September 2014. Google launched its own health-tracking platform, Google Fit, a month later. These platforms allow a myriad of apps to tap into the sensors in smart devices and wearables and, crucially, make sense of the data they collect. Making sense of that data could mean the difference between life and death. Since it launched in 2015, the Apple Watch has periodically made headlines for its life-saving capabilities. Each headline offers a glimpse of Snyder's vision for the future of healthcare.

Right now, much of this health data remains locked away on individual devices – and until doctors and health services are able to access it and process it as standard, it will remain of limited use. But, in the future, a visit to the doctor could involve taking a look at medical records that include wearable data, collected over many years and combined with a detailed personal omics profile. 'It's not meant to replace your physician, it's meant to work with your physician,' says Snyder. Automatic data analysis conducted by algorithms trained on reams of anonymised patient data could also help to spot patterns and outlier patients before they even realise they are ill, referring them to their doctor for further tests and possible treatment.

A version of that future is already available – if you're wealthy enough. In 2015 Snyder co-founded a company called Q Bio, which promises to provide people with a comprehensive picture of their health, based on big data analytics. At $3,500 a visit, it's not cheap, but Snyder is confident the cost will come down considerably over time. And as costs come down, a version of Snyder's omics profiling could become the new standard for healthcare providers, transforming doctors' surgeries from places we visit when we get sick to places we visit to keep us healthy. And while the current cost of personalised healthcare is prohibitive, it may not take very long to come down. 'The goal is to scale it,' says Snyder, 'That's the hope: that we can scale this to the world.'

It won't be easy. In April 2019 Seattle-based genetic-testing and personal health-coaching start-up Arivale shut down, citing a huge void between the cost of providing its service and what customers were willing or able to pay for it. When it launched in 2015, Arivale's flagship programme cost $3,500 a year – but by the time it closed most of its customers were paying a $99 a month subscription for genetic testing and health-coaching. Still, more than $1,000 a year put it out of reach of most people. Despite that, it raised more than $50 million in its lifetime – and proponents of the future that it struggled to sell continue to believe in the benefits of precision medicine. The Global Wellness Institute, an industry body, estimates that the global preventative and personalised medicine industry is already worth upwards of $575 billion. But that's small fry compared to global health spending, which is expected to top $18 trillion by the year 2040. To gain a substantial chunk of the market, precision medicine will need to bring patient numbers up and costs down.

The other barriers to scaling precision medicine are more challenging than shifting public opinion. 'In the US, no one pays to keep you healthy. As the head of one hospital told me, "I don't get paid unless someone walks in the door." So we need to incentivise the system,' says Snyder. That's something over which he and others working in the field have little control – healthcare systems are conservative by nature, and change can often be slow. But there is another major barrier that Snyder has his eye on: the understanding and processing of patient data. 'It needs to be presented in a way that you and your physician can understand,' he says. He compares it to a car, which might have 400 sensors under the bonnet. 'But they don't have 400 displays on the dashboard. And that's how I see medicine in the future. Most physicians don't know how to read a pathology report, but they know how to read a summary. We're collecting all kinds of sophisticated information, pulling it back, getting it processed into a fashion that both the physician and the consumer can understand.' Get that part wrong and the data risks becoming overwhelming or meaningless, even if it is accurate.

Such detailed and instantaneous access to healthcare information – on devices as ubiquitous as smartphones – has left Snyder open to criticism that his vision of the future will create a sort of mass hypochondria. 'Each person should get to decide how much information they want,' he says. Though there's a caveat. If, say, someone has a genetic mutation that puts them at higher risk of cancer, Snyder argues it is better that person knows that information. 'I think it's so valuable, but it has to be used appropriately.' Snyder describes his cohort of 108 patients as 'eager beavers' – but even then, careful consideration had to be given to how findings from the study were communicated, especially when one patient was found to have a potentially incurable genetic mutation. 'We did relay that information back, because they wanted to know,' he says. 'Ignoring data that can help people is really bad. And that's kind of what we do now.'

The other side of the data-collection issue is ownership and control. Accounting firm Ernst & Young estimates that patient data held by Britain's NHS alone could unlock £9.6 billion in annual operational savings and medical benefits for patients. The value here isn't just in the data itself, but in how it can be used. In the coming years it's estimated that the total number of NHS patient records that include whole-genome sequences will increase from the current 100,000 to more than five million. With patient consent, this data can be analysed by approved third parties. 'The number-one thing that people hit me with is privacy: who owns the data?' says Snyder. 'In my view the person owns the data. Everyone owns their own data.' But the reality is more complex. As the still-unfolding history of the information age shows, our personal data might be owned by us, but we have very little control over it. Facebook, for example, might insist that you own your data, but the company considers any insights gleaned from it to be its property. The same goes for Google, whose parent company, Alphabet, owns DeepMind, one of the world's leading AI research companies that specialises in the analysis of healthcare data. Then there's the Chan Zuckerberg Initiative, founded by Facebook CEO Mark Zuckerberg and his wife Priscilla Chan in 2016, which has the goal of curing all diseases in our lifetime.

Silicon Valley's interest in healthcare shouldn't come as a surprise. These companies, built on data, are simply chasing the next big hit. According to analysis by Ernst & Young, a single electronic patient record is worth a little over £100, while the records held by genomic-data aggregators such as Ancestry and 23andMe are valued at £1,500 per person. But these companies only analyse genome samples, not whole sequences, making the potential value much higher. Estimates for the value of electronic patient records combined with genomic data top out at £5,000 per patient. If the healthcare data of today is a goldmine, then the healthcare data of the future is something else entirely. And the great data haul is only just getting started.

CHAPTER THREE

Understanding the body, cell by cell

A cell is an amazing thing. The smallest unit of life, cells were discovered in 1665 by English polymath Robert Hooke, who named them after the small, box-like structures in which Christian monks lived and meditated. Without these tiny boxes of cytoplasm encased in protective membranes, there would be no life. Cells emerged on Earth at least 3.5 billion years ago and have given life to everything from single-cell bacteria to humans. Your brain alone is made up of 80 billion cells. But despite their ubiquity, our understanding of the cells within our own bodies is limited.

In October 2016 a global collaboration of scientists announced a project to collect an unprecedented volume of data. The Human Cell Atlas has a remarkable aim: to create a comprehensive reference map of every human cell. That doesn't mean a map of 37 trillion cells – your body is made up of thousands of different cell types and cell states, with many of them occurring more than once. Instead the project is working through the organs, tissues and systems that make up the human body. Sarah Teichmann, head of cellular genetics at the Wellcome Sanger Institute and co-founder and principal leader of the Human Cell Atlas, likens the work to looking at Google Maps. Right now, much of our understanding of human cells and tissues is equivalent in resolution to zooming right out to view a whole continent. Teichmann is aiming to get that resolution down to Street View level, so that scientists can instead look at a single house – or a single cell – in crystal-clear resolution. To do this, the Human Cell Atlas is using single-cell genomics and spatial genomics, breakthrough technologies that have been developed and scaled over the last decade, to zoom right in and work out exactly what the different types of cell in the human body do.

The traditional way of identifying cell types – essentially checking their shape under a microscope – is painstakingly slow. It's also incredibly limited, as it only allows scientists to discern the difference between, say, a muscle cell and bone cell. But muscle cells alone encompass many different cell types: some muscle cells help you walk or wave, others make your organs ripple and pulsate. With a limited resolution comes a limited understanding.

Think of it in terms of fruit smoothies and fruit salads. Our current view of cells relies on looking at hundreds of thousands of cells at once to measure their gene expression values. In turn, this helps scientists create a picture of cellular function. This method is, as it sounds, somewhat imprecise. It's basically a mush – much like a smoothie. Single-cell genomics enables scientists to profile each and every piece of fruit in isolation: each strawberry, raspberry, banana and blueberry. Combine that with spatial genomics – which tells you, for example, that a banana is next to a strawberry – and you start to build up not just a detailed picture of what pieces of fruit you have, but also how they interact with and affect the other pieces of fruit nearby. From a mush to an elegantly arranged fruit salad, the Human Cell Atlas aims to give a comprehensive view of our cell and tissue architecture. It will do for cells and tissues what the Human Genome Project did for DNA – create a reference map against which each and every one of us can be compared.

'Think about the skin,' Teichmann says, giving an example of a type of tissue we already know a great deal about. 'It consists of different layers.' Towards the bottom of our skin tissue, small round basal cells are created. Here, they divide and push themselves up to the surface of the skin, where they replace old, dead cells, which are then shed. 'If we didn't understand that simple tissue architecture, we wouldn't really understand the function,' Teichmann explains. But many other cell types and tissues remain a mystery. Take the endometrium, for example. This is the mucous membrane that lines the uterus and thickens during the menstrual cycle to prepare for the possible arrival of an embryo. 'Very little was known about the endometrium before the Human Cell Atlas,' she says. 'There are things that have been studied a lot and then there are nooks and crannies that haven't been studied in a lot of detail.' Understanding the tissue architecture of the endometrium will help to explain how it changes throughout a woman's lifetime – periodically during menstruation and pregnancy, but also over the course of many decades. This, in turn, will help to explain what specific cells and cell neighbourhoods are associated with ageing and disease.

In September 2020 researchers working on the Atlas published the results of the first cellular map of the human heart. Using healthy hearts from 14 donors, they studied nearly 500,000 individual cells to work out exactly which genes were switched on in each cell. The research revealed major variations in the types of cell and cell behaviour in different areas of the heart, information that will help explain how a healthy heart develops and could one day pave the way for the creation of more targeted, successful treatments for cardiovascular disease. Cell by cell, tissue by tissue, organ by organ, the human body is being mapped in unprecedented detail. And, even at an early stage, this research is already delivering astonishing results.

On 31 December 2019 the Wuhan Municipal Health Commission in Wuhan, Hubei province, China, reported a cluster of 27 pneumonia cases, the cause of which was unknown. The only link was to Wuhan's Huanan Seafood Wholesale Market, a fish and live-animal market, which was shut down the following day. Patients had a range of symptoms: fever, a dry cough, difficulty breathing – seven of the first wave of patients had severe symptoms. On 9 January 2020 a novel coronavirus, later named SARS-CoV-2 – the virus behind Covid-19 – was found to be the cause of the pneumonia. One day later the genome of SARS-CoV-2 was sequenced and made publicly available by Chinese scientists. On 11 January a 61-year-old man became the first person to die from this mysterious new illness. At the time Chinese authorities said there was no evidence of human-to-human transmission. Two weeks later, on 23 January, the entire city of Wuhan, with more than 11 million people, was put under lockdown. At this point 17 people had died.

Battling the greatest health emergency in a generation, the world has faced a dichotomy. To slow the spread of Covid-19, billions of people were placed under an economically and socially disastrous lockdown. This crude method of disease control can trace its history back to the fifteenth century, when Italian city-states established quarantines to isolate those sick with the plague. Despite almost unimaginable scientific and technological progress in the intervening centuries, when faced with the latest pandemic we once again resorted to medieval means. And yet, in many other ways, the response to the Covid-19 pandemic has enabled us to glimpse the near future of healthcare. As well as the rapid sequencing of its genome, researchers working on the Human Cell Atlas project have also revealed how, cell by cell, Covid-19 attacks the human body. In combination, this work is enabling the development of treatments, containment strategies and vaccines at remarkable speed.

'The first question you ask is, what happens when the virus engages with the host? And then you ask what happens when the host is infected,' says Aviv Regev, a computational biologist and co-leader of the Human Cell Atlas, who is currently head of research and early development at the biotechnology division of Swiss pharmaceutical giant Roche. Just weeks after the discovery of Covid-19, Regev and her colleagues were using data gathered by the Human Cell Atlas to compile a list of all the cells that might be infected by the virus. To do this, they looked at two things: data gathered from the tissue of people not infected with Covid-19 and data gathered from people with the disease. 'At first it was questions about transmission: which cells get infected first?' says Regev. 'Then there's the question of pathogenesis: what's the span of places in the body that the virus could possibly target? Then there were questions of epidemiology: why are older people more susceptible to severe disease compared to younger people and children? And then, once the virus infects, it infects particular cells: do these cells explain why, in some individuals, this disease takes such a ridiculously aggressive course? We took all of these questions and we took the Atlas and we tried to answer it. And we got some pretty good answers.'

In order to get these answers, researchers had to identify the molecules that Covid-19 uses to infect a host. Covid-19 bonds to a receptor molecule that is attached to the surface of many types of cells in the human body, including the heart, gut and lungs. This molecule, ACE2, helps regulate blood pressure, inflammation and the healing of wounds. But for the virus to really enter a cell, it needs additional molecules known as accessory proteases. The Atlas revealed that there are multiple accessory proteases, which helps to explain why Covid-19 is so infectious.

Regev and her colleagues looked at 25 different tissues collected from people not infected with Covid-19.

'We looked at the gut, the liver, the lung, the nasal passages, the eye, the heart, the pancreas, the bladder, the testes, the prostate, the kidneys, the brain, the mammary tissue, blood and bone marrow, tonsils, skin, adipose tissue, peritoneal tissue, bone, lymph nodes, various tumours and ovaries,' she says. In their first analysis alone they looked at 750 samples and four million cells. Their research revealed that Covid-19 could, in theory, lodge itself in cells within the gut, liver, nasal passages and airways, eyes, pancreas, bladder, testes, prostate, kidneys, brain and placenta. 'When we got these results there were no reported neurological symptoms,' Regev explains. 'Today, there are.'

Time after time Regev's findings backed up what frontline doctors were seeing in critically ill patients. 'It's a view of the body we've never had before,' she says. 'It goes into the specific cells and in each of these tissues.' In the lung and heart and some other organs, Regev and her team discovered cells that could be infected with Covid-19 that were related to blood vessels. In hospitals, where severely ill patients were suffering from leaking and clotting blood vessels, the findings were confirmed. The research also helped to explain the age conundrum. 'In extremely young children – from newborn to three years old – the level of ACE2 in the lung, especially the depths of the lung where severe disease happens, is extraordinarily low to non-existent. Whereas in older people it is substantially higher,' she says. So while children can get infected, with Covid-19 most likely attaching itself to cells in the nasal passages and the gut, they are unlikely to get severely ill, because it struggles to reach deep into their lungs.

With the first stage of the study complete, Regev and her colleagues moved on to looking at samples collected from people infected with Covid-19. This enabled them to track the progress of the virus through the body. They collected blood and tissue samples from the lining of people's airways and, finally, autopsy studies. These samples were combined to form the first ever single-cell analysis of tissue from severely ill Covid-19 patients. And it was here that the Atlas data started to really show its worth. 'We can actually see cells that are infected,' says Regev. 'We can detect the viral RNA inside cells. That allows you to look at two cells in the same individual, one of which has the virus and another that does not. We can compare them and see what the virus is doing to the cells. This helps physicians and biologists who want to understand viral infection, but also drug developers who want to develop better therapies.'

Understanding how Covid-19 infects individual cells is also crucial to understanding what treatments won't work against it. Early in the pandemic the antimalarial drug hydroxychloroquine was put forward as a potential treatment for the disease. The fervour was based on a study that showed the drug had an inhibitory effect on a specific enzyme that allows Covid-19 to enter lung cells. The catch? The cells being studied were derived from the kidneys of the African green monkey. Use of so-called Vero cells in scientific research is common – but when it came to Covid-19, it led scientists and policymakers down the wrong path. When the experiment was eventually repeated on human cells, hydroxychloroquine did nothing to prevent the virus from entering. It was a dead end. That conclusion was reached only after an enormous amount of time and money had been spent on clinical trials and research. The US alone stockpiled 31 million hydroxychloroquine pills for the treatment of Covid-19. They were all useless.

The data that Regev and her colleagues have compiled for the Atlas could, in the near future, enable doctors assessing patients with Covid-19 to make better decisions. A physician analysing a blood sample would be able to hone in on specific biomarkers. 'Once you've done this kind of study, you can show that we should actually be measuring the levels of specific genes with very high precision.' Blood analysed, a doctor would then be able to ascertain that, faced with two almost identical patients of the same age and with the same risk characteristics, one will likely get better quite quickly, while another might soon take a dramatic turn for the worse. 'That's what high-resolution data allows you to do,' says Regev. 'You can take two individuals that, by standard clinical measures, look very similar and better predict the future.' For drug developers, too, it is providing more detailed information on targets for treatments and vaccines, and explaining cell by cell how our immune systems could be harnessed to beat the virus. Vaccine development normally takes a decade or longer. Faced with Covid-19, various candidates will enter production inside a year.

Expand that process beyond Covid-19 and you begin to understand the crucial role single-cell data will play in the healthcare systems of the future. 'Unlike your genome, which is kind of stationary, your cells change all the time,' says Regev. Even today, a trip to the doctor might involve giving a saliva, urine or blood sample. What single-cell data will change is what doctors can learn from taking these samples. 'The technologies that we use – single-cell genomics, the spatial methods for atlassing tissue sections – in ten, twenty years, they'll be used for diagnostics,' says Teichmann. 'So when you take a blood sample, instead of doing a blood count, you'll do single-cell genomics of the blood.' This will turn routine check-ups into an opportunity to collect vast quantities of actionable patient data, spotting the signs of disease earlier and prescribing better courses of treatment, based on individual requirements rather than population-based assumptions. 'Our cells carry within them not just the impact of our genome, but of everything that happens to us,' says Regev. 'They tell us something about what is going on with us right now, and possibly what is going to happen in the future. Over time, this data will become just as important as, and possibly in some cases more important than, our genomic information.'

Much as it has wrought havoc on healthcare systems and economies across the globe, Covid-19 has also shown a way forward – and the acute need for a more personalised approach to medicine. 'We got to see the extent of variation in how humans interact with one variable,' says Regev. Genetically, Covid-19 has changed very little as it has spread across the world. But, in infecting people of all ages and races, the disease has laid bare the variation between humans, and shown the flaws in a one-size-fits-all approach to healthcare. 'It's the world's largest and saddest clinical trial. But the one thing we can do with it is try to do our absolute best to improve for the future,' says Regev. 'It's played out completely differently in different individuals. And we have to know why, if we want to control it.'

While organisations like the Human Cell Atlas are providing more data for analysis, others are building new ways of interpreting that data. At BenevolentAI, a London-based start-up that uses artificial intelligence for drug discovery, Covid-19 was a major test of its technology. BenevolentAI's systems are designed to find new targets for drug development by searching through vast troves of academic papers and scientific literature to make connections that humans alone have missed. Faced with Covid-19, the researchers at BenevolentAI had to recalibrate the system to look for a potential treatment that already existed – a so-called 'off-label use' for a drug that was approved for use in humans.

'We can find new connections,' says Alix Lacoste, vice-president of data science at BenevolentAI. 'It would take a human a really long time, because you have to sift through billions of interactions. But a machine is a lot faster.' These interactions are chunks of information on a vast database known as a knowledge graph – essentially a collection of more than a billion relationships between genes, targets, diseases, proteins and drugs. To search this database, BenevolentAI's researchers use a toolbox of specially trained AI assistants with the uncanny knack of finding needles in a veritable haystack of pharmaceutical data. The premise is simple: among the troves of academic papers and literature there must be scores of significant discoveries that have been forgotten about or overlooked. Put an AI to work on that data, however, and new discoveries will reveal themselves.

BenevolentAI uses natural language processing not only to spot keywords in academic and pharmaceutical data, but also to understand their meaning and context. This lets the company look deep within the data, creating detailed maps of disease, genes, biological processes and potential treatments. For Covid-19, Lacoste and her colleagues worked with Peter Richardson, BenevolentAI's vice-president of pharmacology, to analyse data for possible connections to the disease. Once the system understood what Covid-19 was – and how it attacked the human body – it could start looking for links between the disease and specific genes.

But rather than being automated, BenevolentAI's work on Covid-19 has been deliberately collaborative. 'It will find links from really far away in the knowledge graph,' says Lacoste. 'But, on the other hand, it can make a lot of dumb decisions. So when you have a human in the loop, they can add their expertise and creativity.' With humans and AI working in collaboration, Lacoste and her colleagues quickly uncovered a promising candidate for treating patients infected with Covid-19: baricitinib, an anti-inflammatory drug made by American pharmaceutical company Eli Lilly. In November 2020, the FDA granted baricitinib an emergency use authorisation for treating people hospitalised with Covid-19. Without the AI's all-seeing eye, it is unlikely researchers would have spotted baricitinib's potential.

The work on Covid-19 gives a snapshot of the potential benefits of using AI systems to aid drug discovery. The key, explains Lacoste, is how wide an AI can open its eyes. 'The pharma industry tends to look locally. They're typically organised by therapeutic area,' she says. An AI, by contrast, makes leaps that no human mind ever could. 'One of the first machine learning algorithms that we developed is called tensor factorisation. That's kind of how Netflix recommendations work. It's basically representing every user and every film in a matrix,' says Lacoste. In that matrix you have two people, both of whom like the same four action films. If the first person then watches and enjoys a fifth action film, chances are the second person will like it as well. 'We take a similar approach to understanding genes and diseases. Essentially we're able to find similarities between diseases or genes or drugs in a similar way to how you find similarities between films or film lovers.' That's a simplified example, but the principle is similar. As well as Covid-19, BenevolentAI's technology has already been used to develop potential new treatments for Parkinson's disease and motor neurone disease, both of which have entered clinical trials. The breakthroughs were the result of identifying novel compounds not previously associated with the respective diseases.

The promise of such a system is that it helps to save not only lives, but also time and money. Drug discovery is an expensive and time-consuming business. That expense locks promising new treatments away behind eye-wateringly high drug prices, while also making pharmaceutical companies notoriously conservative. The average cost of getting a new drug approved is $2.6 billion, with nine out of every ten drug candidates failing to win regulatory approval. Focus on drugs targeting Alzheimer's disease, and that failure rate jumps to 99.6 per cent. 'One of the key ways to limit failure is to find new avenues of research,' says Lacoste. Increased use of AI systems in drug discovery should bring the failure rates down, both by finding better targets for treatments and then by improving the treatments themselves. If you pick the right target to begin with, you can eliminate failures before they get too expensive. And that's what most of BenevolentAI's machine learning systems are focused on: finding errors early and squashing them. 'Pharma tends to go after the same targets,' says Lacoste. 'AI systems can find new approaches.'

CHAPTER FOUR

A cure for cancer

By the time he was 15 years old Connor McMahon had already beaten cancer twice. Connor, a talented young hockey player who grew up in Cumming, a small city just north of Atlanta, Georgia, had spent 12 years of his life fighting acute lymphoblastic leukaemia. He had endured six years of chemotherapy, been hospitalised eight times, spent eight weeks as a hospital inpatient, attended 136 cancer-centre appointments, had four surgeries, 23 bone-marrow aspirations, 40 spinal taps and had taken thousands of pills. But, by the summer of 2015, Connor was out the other side. He received his last dose of chemotherapy and sailed through subsequent blood tests to check if the cancer had returned. Month after month the blood tests came back perfect. Then, in June 2016, abnormalities were detected. More tests. Then the phone rang.

'His oncologist called me,' says Don, Connor's father. 'He said, "There's no good way to tell you this, but the cancer's back." I was in denial.' The prognosis was not good. The only option for Connor was a bone-marrow transplant, which would give him a 30 per cent chance of surviving the next 12 months. 'When the head of oncology at the best children's hospital in the south tells you your kid's going to be dead in twelve months, it kinda hurts,' says Don. 'He said, "It's not about quantity, it's about quality. There's really nothing we can do." I was devastated.'

More bad news would follow. Tests confirmed that six years of chemotherapy had left Connor sterile. That night Don was having some drinks at a neighbour's house when his phone started pinging. He was being bombarded with messages from someone who followed 'Connor's Hope', a Facebook page that he had created to document his son's journey and shine a light on children going through similarly hard times. When Don woke up the next morning and looked at a video he had been sent the night before, his hangover quickly lifted. The video showed a child just like Connor, months from death, who had been given an experimental treatment to fight her cancer. Like Connor, the girl in the video had acute lymphoblastic leukaemia, the most common childhood cancer. And from the brink of death, the girl in the video had, within days, been declared cancer-free. 'I walked into Connor's room and I woke him up and we watched the video and he said, "I want that."'

The girl in the video was Emily Whitehead. Like Connor, Emily was one of the unlucky kids with acute lymphoblastic leukaemia. Remission rates for the most common form of the disease are 85 per cent. Emily and Connor found themselves on the wrong side of the divide. Like Connor, Emily's cancer was ferocious. For 16 months it resisted chemotherapy. At its peak, the cancer in her bloodstream was doubling with each passing day. A bone-marrow transplant was no longer possible – the aggressiveness of the chemotherapy that had failed to defeat Emily's cancer had, in the process, almost defeated

Emily. Her parents were told it was terminal. She was six years old.

Like so many in their position, Emily's parents refused to accept their daughter's fate. But every avenue of research resulted in the same conclusion: there was nothing that could be done. That was until they heard about a clinical trial that could turn Emily's immune system into a powerful weapon against her cancer. In April 2012 Emily was enrolled as the first paediatric patient in the clinical trial of an experimental new immunotherapy treatment called CAR-T cell therapy. The therapy, led by a clinical team at the University of Pennsylvania, had never been tested in a child before, and there were doubts it would be able to keep up with the rapid, violent nature of Emily's leukaemia. But it was her only hope.

The therapy is at the very cutting edge of synthetic biology. It's the world's first living drug – a scientific breakthrough that reprogrammed Emily's immune cells into ferocious cancer-killers. To do this, millions of Emily's

T cells – which form part of a group of white blood cells known as lymphocytes – were removed. Doctors then inserted new genetic instructions. The technique uses a modified but deactivated version of HIV as a vehicle to deliver its payload. The use of HIV is a no-brainer: the virus is ruthlessly effective at targeting T cells. It normally reprograms them to produce more HIV, shutting down the immune system. But what makes HIV a killer can also make it a life-saver. Modified as a delivery vehicle for CAR-T, the virus infected Emily's T cells with new genetic instructions that told them to target CD19, a protein found on the surface of cancerous B cells, and kill them. These engineered T cells, known as chimeric antigen receptor cells (hence CAR-T cell therapy) are then put back into the patient's bloodstream. The name is a nod to the chimera, the monstrous fire-breathing hybrid creature of Greek mythology that combines a lion, a goat and a serpent. In this case scientists had created a molecular chimera: an antibody on the outside of the cell, and T-cell signalling domains on the inside, all wrapped up inside a shell of HIV.

Except that this isn't really a drug at all. A drug, in the traditional sense, is inert. It enters your body, does something and fades away. The effect is temporary. CAR-T is alive. If all goes to plan, each of these killer T cells can take out 10,000 cancer cells. The body turns into a warzone as the patient's immune system launches an all-out attack on the cancer. This is the very definition of precision, personalised medicine: a patient's own cells, re-engineered to kill the cancer that has taken over their bodies, potentially giving them a second chance at life when almost all hope is lost.

Within days of receiving the treatment at the Children's Hospital of Philadelphia, Emily had a dangerously high fever, just one symptom of a cytokine storm – a potentially deadly side-effect of CAR-T, caused by the flood of natural chemicals released from her immune cells as they were activated to destroy the cancer. Her temperature hit 41.1°C (106°F). She was on a ventilator for two weeks, in a coma and fighting for her life. Her family and friends came to her bedside to say goodbye. Then, at the last moment, a blood test revealed an abnormally large increase in one of her cytokines. An urgent call was put out to the hospital's pharmacy for an immunosuppressant drug called tocilizumab – normally a treatment for rheumatoid arthritis – to try and bring Emily's immune system under control. Within hours she began to stabilise. Then, on her seventh birthday, Emily woke up. Eight days later she was declared cancer-free. Emily is now 15 and still cancer-free.

In October 2016 Connor enrolled in the same clinical trial as Emily at Duke University Children's Hospital in Durham, North Carolina. And, like Emily, he got a dangerously high fever. 'He spiked a fever on day one,' says Don. 'By day two it was 104. Then it went to 105. Then to 106. It topped out at 107.2 and it stayed there for three days. He was hallucinating, he was hysterical. And then his fever broke. In less than a day it went from 107.2 to 98.7. The next day he was up and walking.' Like Emily, within days of receiving the treatment Connor was cancer-free. Thirty days later the hockey fanatic was back out on the ice. The treatment's success on children was crucial. CAR-T was so powerful and so experimental that there were concerns it could be too ferocious to control. But then came Emily and Connor – and suddenly the breakthrough treatment had a chance to go mainstream.

In June 2017 Don flew to Washington DC to speak in front of an FDA panel that would decide whether or not to approve CAR-T. If they did, it would become the first ever FDA-approved gene therapy. 'When I was done speaking, the entire panel was in tears,' Don recalls. 'Connor has truly been one of the pioneers of this.' On 30 August 2017 the FDA approved Kymriah, the brand name for cancer therapy that had been developed at the University of Pennsylvania. The therapy is now licensed to the Swiss pharmaceutical giant Novartis and is approved in the US for the treatment of acute lymphoblastic leukaemia in children and young adults. In 2018 it was also approved for use in the European Union. But that approval is just the end of the latest chapter in the remarkable story of how our immune systems have been turned into cancer-killers.

That story began in the early 1990s when Carl June and Bruce Levine, co-creators of CAR-T, experimentally treated HIV patients using a version of the virus that had been re-engineered to alter the DNA of T cells. They were then working at the Naval Medical Research Institute in Bethesda, Maryland. June and Levine's breakthrough stopped the virus from replicating, which, in turn, boosted the immune function of people infected with HIV. Even then the potential to use a similar technique to treat blood cancers was obvious – if tantalisingly out of reach. It would take almost two decades for the rest of the scientific community to take the idea seriously.

In August 2011 June and Levine reported remarkable results from the first trials of their experimental cancer-killing T-cell therapy. Similarly to Emily and Connor, who would be the first children enrolled in the clinical trials, the first three adult patients all had chronic lymphocytic leukaemia, another cancer that affects white blood cells. After failing to respond to more traditional therapies, two of the three patients made miraculous recoveries after receiving

CAR-T. Nine years later, two of those patients remain cancer-free. The third died soon after receiving CAR-T, but might have survived had treatment begun sooner.

Like all treatments for cancer, CAR-T isn't perfect. Around the same time as Emily made her remarkable recovery, another child slipped away. A ten-year-old girl, who also had acute lymphoblastic leukaemia and was also treated at the Children's Hospital of Philadelphia, initially responded well to CAR-T but relapsed two months later. Her cancer had mutated and the killer T cells were unable to stop it. She died of her disease.

Much as traditional cancer treatments are almost brutally imprecise, CAR-T is ruthlessly targeted. Using the patient's own cells makes it unlikely that the treatment will be rejected, while the nature of the immune fire-storm it unleashes means that hospital stays are shorter in comparison to years of chemotherapy. For Connor, CAR-T lasted just three months, involved four days of chemotherapy, three hospitalisations, ten days as an in-patient, fewer than 20 appointments, two surgeries, three bone-marrow aspirations, three spinal taps and fewer than 200 pills. It also delivered long-lasting results. Connor is now 19 and has been cancer-free for four years. Results from clinical trials of Kymriah released in 2018 show that 76 per cent of the cancer patients survived for a year or more – something unheard of with other treatments. Before CAR-T, children like Emily and Connor had a near-zero per cent survival rate. The estimated survival rate now tops 83 per cent.

Cancer is the second-leading cause of death globally – one in six of us will die of the disease. In 2010, the last year for which figures are available, the total annual economic cost of cancer was $1.16 trillion. In the UK alone, 2.5 million people are currently living with cancer. That number will hit four million by 2030. Advances in the fight against cancer have been rapid. In the 1970s the median survival time after diagnosis was one year. Now it is more than ten years. In the effort to push that number higher still – and cure some forms of cancer – immunotherapy is seen as a crucial weapon.

'The patients and the families feel empowered by using their own immune systems, albeit re-engineered, to fight off their cancer,' says Levine, who is now professor in cancer gene therapy at the University of Pennsylvania. 'They place their faith and hope in us. It's like being an astronaut. You get loaded up in this capsule, this clinical trial, and it's kind of like getting shot up into space. And hopefully you'll come back, but it's not a sure thing. These really are our pioneers. These are our astronauts of twenty-first-century medicine.' But a trip into space and back doesn't come cheap. Kymriah carries a $475,000 price tag for one person's course of treatment – a small price for another shot at life, but prohibitively expensive for widespread use. And so, with FDA approval for Kymriah secured, Levine is now focused on pushing the potential of personal cancer treatment further still. And that means scaling up.

The challenges here, as with so many personalised treatments, are numerous. For a start, the economic model is backwards. Big pharmaceutical companies are, for the most part, familiar with developing products like Viagra or Humira, where exactly the same drug is used by millions of people to treat the same conditions. With Kymriah, it's the opposite. For one, it's not really a drug, it's a bag of genetically engineered cells that's unique to each patient. And then there are the challenges of making it. Each course of Kymriah takes, on average, 21 days to manufacture, a labour-intensive and incredibly specialist process that can only be completed at a handful of laboratories around the world.

Levine is also the founding director of the Clinical Cell and Vaccine Production Facility at the University of Pennsylvania, a position that focuses on assessing new technologies and manufacturing techniques for CAR-T. A key to that is automation – something made devilishly hard by the sheer complexity of turning a patient's cells into cancer-killers. First, blood is drawn. It's then spun in a centrifuge to split the T cells from the rest. The T cells are then cryogenically frozen and shipped to a Novartis facility in New Jersey, where they are re-engineered.

Once the process is complete, the T cells are cryogenically frozen once more, shipped back to the hospital, thawed and administered to the patient. 'There's a lot of work going on in automation,' says Levine. This could bring with it three big benefits: greater precision, greater speed and reduced cost. Greater precision should mean a more potent therapy, while greater speed and reduced cost would make CAR-T available to more patients. In terms of expense, the single most costly element of the process is manufacturing the modified HIV virus that is used as the delivery vehicle for the therapy. To overcome this, breakthroughs in gene-editing technologies such as CRISPR could remove the need for a viral vehicle altogether. Improvements are also being made in the chimeric antigen receptor – the CAR in CAR-T – to make it more potent. Researchers are also hunting for clues to understand why some patients respond well to CAR-T while others don't.

Scaling up manufacturing and increasing potency become even more important when it comes to using

CAR-T on solid cancers, rather than just cancers of the blood. 'There are a number of challenges with solid cancers,' says Levine. In blood cancers CD19, the protein that CAR-T hunts for, is an ideal target. It's relatively easy to find, only expressed on B cells and not found on any other tissue. The only major side-effect is that, in targeting cancerous B cells, CAR-T also targets healthy B cells. Thankfully, with follow-up treatment, people can live long and happy lives without B cells. 'In solid cancers it's very difficult to find a similar target,' says Levine. That's because almost every other cancer target isn't expressed on every tumour cell – or the target is also expressed on healthy tissues that we can't survive without. Compared to cancers of the bone marrow and blood, other forms of the disease are better at hiding. 'You can have a potent anti-tumour effect, but you also have significant off-target side-effects.' If finding the right target is hard, then it's a whole other challenge to get to it. Solid cancers are, by their very nature, solid. Blood cancers can be approached from any angle, which makes delivery of the re-engineered T cells more straightforward. But solid cancers are encased within fortresses. 'You have to get inside the tumour,' says Levine. 'It can be like peeling away the layers of an onion.' A number of research groups are now on the hunt for other targetable antigens, potentially expanding the scope of T-cell attacks to the pancreatic, ovarian, breast and prostate cancers that claim millions of lives a year.

Progress is being made at a remarkable rate. Since 2017 the CAR-T industry has exploded. There are close to 400 CAR-T companies worldwide, with hundreds of clinical trials being conducted to further the scope and precision of the therapy. In clinical trials at the University of Pennsylvania Children's Hospital alone, more than 700 patients have now been treated with CAR-T. Across the world, that number is in the thousands. And capacity is increasing all the time.

Until the landmark 2011 study, cancer immunotherapy was seen as something of a joke by the research community. Now it is seen as a potential cure for multiple forms of the disease. This is only possible because the scientific community has come to understand, in brutal detail, why cancer is such a potent killer. For so many of us, cancer comes as a surprise – a deadly disease that dodges our immune systems and can remain undetected for years. When you catch the common cold, you get a runny nose and a headache. You spike a fever. That's all a result of your immune system kicking in. When you get cancer, your immune system does nothing. This is a disease that uses every trick in the book to disable or hide from our immune response. This makes early diagnosis hard, with treatment often a brutal combination of poisons that are unable to differentiate between cancerous cells and healthy tissue. Cancer dodges T cells before they can act – all the while hiding in plain sight. CAR-T removes that cover, dragging cancer cells into the open and destroying them using the power of our own immune systems.

In the future, breakthroughs in the field will enable doctors to target more forms of the disease with greater precision and potency, with fewer side-effects. Significant challenges remain, however. Gene editing, which could further the power of immunotherapy, is an ethical minefield that society is yet to properly address. 'We have, over the last several decades, been harnessing the power of gene engineering,' says Levine. 'But that power also comes with responsibility.' In 2019 He Jiankui, a Chinese scientist who created the world's first gene-edited babies, was jailed for three years. He was universally condemned when he announced the birth of the babies, twin girls whose embryos had been genetically modified to try and give them protection against HIV. 'The story of He Jiankui shows that these approaches can be co-opted for purposes that are ethically over the border,' says Levine. In an emerging field, he says it is crucial that public perception doesn't get clouded by bad actors. In He's case, the experiment was dangerous because it wasn't precise enough. While He targeted the correct gene, the edit wasn't an exact match for the mutation associated with resistance to HIV. Such imprecision could have dangerous long-term effects. It was a leap too far, too early, conducted with no oversight and in breach of the law. Levine says such high-profile rogue cases risk confusing the way people think about gene editing as a tool for precision medicine. 'I said to one of our patients a couple of years ago, "Have you ever thought of yourself as a GMO [genetically modified organism]? Because now you are."'

In the emerging field of precision, personalised healthcare, Levine and his patients are pioneers. Future iterations of cancer immunotherapy will carry more sophisticated payloads that perform multiple functions to track down the most stubborn and deadly forms of the disease. 'I think the cure is within our own cells,' says Levine. 'The immune system has been evolving for hundreds of millions of years. It's had a head start.'

CHAPTER FIVE

Healing the mind

Remove a brain from a warm, dead body and it quickly falls apart. As the blood drips away, it turns from a light yellowish-pink to a cold, murky grey. The brain becomes acidic and starts to eat itself, as its cells collapse in a process called liquefaction. Alive just minutes ago, the brain is now irreversibly dead. 'For me, as a neuroscientist, that tissue is not functional,' says Sergiu Pasca, associate professor of psychiatry and behavioural sciences at Stanford University. 'I cannot hear those neurons firing, I cannot ask questions about how they're miscommunicating with other neurons.' Even the most meticulously preserved brain tissue – frozen and cut into translucent slices less than 2 millimetres thick – pales in comparison.

The 86 billion neurons and hundreds of trillions of synapses that make us who we are remain, broadly, a mystery. Single neurons and small circuits of neurons are well understood, but such advances have done little to answer seemingly simple questions. How, for example, do many thousands of neurons work together to tell you to smile? How do you look at a cloud and know what it is? And then there are the hard questions: what are the genetics of schizophrenia, autism and other brain disorders? Disorders of the brain affect nearly one-fifth of the world's population and yet, even after decades of research, little to no progress has been made in understanding the molecular causes of psychiatric disorders. 'If you look across branches of medicine, therapeutic success is very often correlated with accessibility to tissue,' says Pasca. He's got a point. Advances in precision medicine have had huge impacts on oncology, for example, where cancerous cells can be both easily accessed and targeted. When it comes to psychology, getting hold of the tissue required to conduct detailed studies is impossible. 'We're not even close to that in psychology,' Pasca says.

And so, with no functional brain tissue to study, Pasca has gone about building it from scratch in the lab. It's nowhere near as ghoulish as it sounds. In 2012 Shinya Yamanaka, a Japanese stem-cell researcher, won the Nobel Prize in Physiology or Medicine for a breakthrough that is seen as one of the foundations of regenerative medicine. Yamanaka showed that it was possible to turn back time and flip fully developed cells back to their egg-like state. 'This was so surprising because we always thought that development was a one-way street,' says Pasca. Yamanaka had found the proteins that could turn a skin cell, for example, into brain cells. The process works by exposing cells to a set of genes that are found in pluripotent stem cells – master cells that give rise to all other cells. When this happens, remarkably, those cells also become pluripotent, meaning that they can differentiate into more than one type of cell or tissue.

Pasca, who was in his last year of medical school when the breakthrough was announced, immediately saw the potential for psychiatry. 'You could take skin cells from patients with psychiatric disorders, reprogram them into pluripotent stem cells and then guide those to become neurons or brain tissue that would allow us to study cellular processes in a non-invasive way. If that isn't precision medicine, I don't know what is.' Pasca, whose clinical expertise is in autism spectrum disorders and early-onset schizophrenia, wondered if he could use this method to re-create neurons from patients with autism and schizophrenia in a non-invasive way, thus enabling him to study the conditions and their effect on the brain in detail.

He worked with cells from people with Timothy syndrome, a rare and often fatal genetic condition that is caused by some of the same gene variants associated with schizophrenia, forms of autism spectrum disorder and bipolar disorder. People with Timothy syndrome are known to have a mutation on a gene that causes their cells to let in too much calcium. Pasca used Yamanaka's breakthrough technique to turn skin cells from people with Timothy syndrome into pluripotent stem cells and then into cortical neurons – the neurons of the cerebral cortex, the most advanced region of the brain. The process not only worked, it also allowed him to study in minute detail the defect in the way cells handled calcium. The research was the cover story of the November 2011 issue of *Nature Medicine*. But the experiment had a limitation: the neurons were stuck at the bottom of a flat Petri dish – in a human brain they would be interconnected in a three-dimensional structure. 'The main limitation was time,' says Pasca. The human brain is constructed over many months – with the development of neurons only complete by 27 weeks of gestation. But Pasca's Petri-dish-bound neurons could only survive for a few weeks, even though the cells were still dividing and being generated at a similar rate. To properly study neurological development, Pasca needed the cells to stick around for months, not days. His solution was to coat the Petri dish with a chemical that didn't allow the cells to lie flat. 'When that happens, they essentially stay in a bowl of cells,' says Pasca. At that point he expected the blob of cells to survive for a few more weeks. Instead it started to self-organise and survived for several months. 'This is the beginning of a revolution in three-dimensional cell cultures,' he says. From studying a flat Petri dish of cells with a limited lifespan, Pasca was now able to study increasingly complex blobs – or, as he refers to them, organoids.

In early experiments these brain organoids were allowed to develop by themselves. Within days, the pluripotent stem cells started to transform into neurons. In less than a month, defined regions of the brain started to form. When studied closely, it became clear that these weren't just rough replicas, but remarkably accurate – albeit simplified – versions of real human brains. The potential here is huge. Many of the processes that guide human-brain development simply don't occur in rodents, making animal studies of limited use when developing new treatments. And organoids can now be nudged and persuaded into certain forms, enabling scientists to re-create specific regions of the developing brain.

While these organoids are complex, their complexity shouldn't be overstated. And don't even think about calling them mini-brains. 'It's incredibly inaccurate,' says Pasca. 'These are not brains. These are not mini versions of brains in a dish.' He prefers to think of his creations as models – a way of gaining access to inaccessible cellular features of brain development and function. The use of cells gathered from patients with genetic variations is also a huge step forward. By creating brain organoids from patients with genetic forms of autism spectrum disorder, for example, it's possible to compare how these organoids develop and behave, when compared to organoids without such mutations. In doing this, Pasca has been able to identify both cause and effect. These organoids – and assembloids, which are collections of different organoids bound together – are already helping to reveal how cells organise during brain development and how that organisation can go wrong. And if Pasca can identify the molecular mechanisms behind these processes, he might be able to find ways to restore them.

'The aim is to show, or not, that this new approach is a way to move us from behavioural psychiatry to molecular, precision-medicine-based psychiatry,' he says.

In a 2017 study, Pasca and his colleagues created two human forebrain organoids. The forebrain is a core part of the developing human brain, which goes on to form regions that control speech, abstract thought, sex drive, blood pressure and hunger. One organoid was developed to replicate a brain region where excitatory neurons are born, and another replicated a region where inhibitory neurons are born. 'This is really thought to be critical for autism spectrum disorders,' says Pasca, but studying this process, which takes place in the developing brain, was previously impossible. Once ready, the organoids were left in a test tube for a couple of days to allow them to fuse together. But they didn't just fuse – they started to communicate and form neural circuits. The inhibitory neurons, which are not born in the cortex but migrate from another region during development, started to jump towards the excitatory neurons. 'Nobody has seen this process before,' says Pasca. In organoids grown from skin cells collected from people with Timothy syndrome, he observed something quite different. The inhibitory cells still jumped, but they did so less efficiently – each jump was shorter than the last. 'They're essentially left behind,' he says. It's a small and hugely significant discovery. Once you understand a molecular process that can cause diseases and disorders, you can potentially develop treatments to target it. 'This is the very beginning of what I like to call molecular psychiatry,' says Pasca.

To progress to the next stage, the organoid revolution needs to move from Petri dish to clinical trial. Pasca gives the example of severely premature babies – those born before 25 weeks, 80 per cent of whom go on to develop moderate-to-severe long-term neurodevelopmental issues. With their lungs not functioning, the brains of severely premature babies are at high risk of not getting enough oxygen to develop properly. The condition cannot be studied in mice, as mice are more resilient to low oxygen than humans – but it can be studied in human brain organoids. In an experiment using organoids, Pasca and his colleagues were able to identify the effects of hypoxia on the developing brain. And they were able to identify a drug that was already in development that could block the malfunction it caused. 'What's the next stage?' Pasca asks. With no animal model, is an organoid model enough? 'Some disorders are so severe, the prognosis is so bad, that one could think that pursuing these clinical trials could be worthwhile.' An alternative would be for an organoid study to identify an already approved drug that could be permitted for off-label use in human trials.

Those first trials – if and when they do arrive – will be crucial in proving the reliability of organoid models as a method of finding potential treatments for brain disorders. 'Many of the major pharma companies have been moving out of neuroscience,' says Pasca. With development costs high and success rates low, the economics of developing new drugs to target psychiatric disorders no longer makes sense. 'In the face of incredible failure, most pharma companies decided to no longer invest,' he explains. Organoids, he hopes, won't just reveal better targets for drug developments, but will also provide better ways to safely test those drugs, thus improving the success rate of human trials and, eventually, delivering more precise, effective treatments for disorders such as autism and schizophrenia. 'Advances in psychiatry and medicine, the biology of these disorders, have been incredibly, incredibly slow,' says Pasca. 'That advance needs to be made.'

The organoid revolution isn't the only way scientists are coming to understand the genes, pathways and underlying mechanisms of psychiatric disorders. In 2015 the National Institute of Mental Health in the US announced an ambitious $50 million project to create a computer model for brain genomics. Like the Human Cell Atlas, this project, known as PsychENCODE, is an attempt to create a vast, publicly available database of the genetic and biological processes active throughout the human brain. Unlike disorders caused by mutations in a single gene, such as cystic fibrosis, most neurological disorders are the result of hundreds of genetic variations and environmental factors, making it hard to pinpoint which factors carry with them the highest risk of disease. Understand the mechanisms, though, and you can start to create intricate maps of cause and effect.

'The paradox of mental illness is that it's actually highly heritable,' says Mark Gerstein, a professor of bioinformatics at Yale University School of Medicine and a lead researcher on the PsychENCODE project. 'It's much more heritable than, say, heart disease and cancer.' The paradox for Gerstein is similar to the issue faced by Pasca: we know many of the genetic variations that put people at higher risk of diseases of the brain, but historically we have had very little understanding of the mechanisms that drive these variations. 'Because people don't have a very good grasp on the molecular mechanism, it's very hard to think about how to design a drug,' says Gerstein. 'If you want to make a drug, you want to make it target a particular protein, or gene, or something that's acting abnormally.'

PsychENCODE's aim is to fill in the blanks. And to do this, you need a lot of dead brains – 1,866 to be precise. The consortium of scientists, spanning 15 different research institutions, analysed a myriad of brain samples, both tissues and single cells, to build up a comprehensive picture of the complex systems that could potentially lead to psychiatric disorders. Data gathered, they then needed to make sense of it. 'Normally when people talk about deep learning or machine learning they think of a black box,' says Gerstein. 'But the way we did it was different – we opened up the black box.' Making petabytes of complex neuroscientific data understandable and interpretable is no small task. To tackle the issue, Gerstein led the development of a deep-learning predictor, an AI system that attempted to calculate the risk of someone having schizophrenia, based on their genetic variations and gene expression levels.

This system isn't intended to make diagnoses, but rather to shine a light on the molecular causes of psychiatric disorders. As it analysed the data, the predictor highlighted what features it saw as important and explained how the areas it had focused on related to specific genes, pathways and cell types that were in turn related to psychiatric disorders. It's like showing your working in maths, albeit on an epic scale. 'It's good at suggesting targets for drugs,' says Gerstein. 'That's the great hope. That people will develop new drugs for these conditions.' And if drugs for psychiatric disorders can be made more targeted – or even designed for an individual's specific condition – they should be better for the people who take them. Globally, the economic burden of mental-health disorders was estimated at $8.5 trillion in 2010, putting it at a similar level to cardiovascular diseases and higher than that of cancer and diabetes. That figure is expected almost to double by 2030. Finding more targeted treatments for both psychiatric disorders such as schizophrenia and mental disorders such as depression could have a profound impact on our society and our economy.

PsychENCODE's initial work, published in 2018, only gave Gerstein and his colleagues part of the picture.

Over the coming years the consortium of scientists is zooming in further still, to understand the role of individual cells in how the human brain functions. To do this they will once again create a gargantuan map, this time of cells, to show where specific cell types are located in the brain and reveal how prevalent they are. The final hurdle is to understand how this prevalence of cell types relates to genetic variations. This extra detail will be crucial in understanding, at the most minute of levels, the processes that make some people more at risk of developing psychiatric disorders. 'People say, "Oh, you have this particular condition – maybe this gene is on more." That can be true, but it's a bit more indirect,' says Gerstein. The consortium's analysis aims to show that a higher prevalence of certain cells is the key process that drives genetic variance in the brain. 'That's particularly important in neuroscience because we have so many different types of cell in the brain,' Gerstein says.

Higher-resolution studies will create even more data. And this data deluge presents a challenge. 'Machine learning is kind of a buzzword right now,' says Gerstein. 'These models are cool and people like them, but they're not very satisfying.' Or, to put it another way, scientists concerned with understanding the causes of disease don't learn much by teaching a machine how to do a clever trick. 'It doesn't provide you with much scientific understanding. It might be nice when you're trying to recognise a canary versus a hawk in computer vision, but if you're a scientist you really want to understand it – particularly if you want to treat a patient or design a drug.'

Making that work in practice is a major challenge for personalised healthcare. Think of it like this. In the coming years you may visit your doctor with a health complaint. To make a diagnosis, your doctor will look at your omics profiles and compare, say, your blood sample against a vast global database of biomarkers for disease. Data will be crunched and the machine will be spit out a diagnosis at the other end. Question is: how did the machine make the decision? 'If you're a scientist, you really want to understand it,' says Gerstein. When it comes to PsychENCODE's work to map individual cells in the human brain, that means building computational models that can grapple with huge quantities of data successfully, but then also explain why it made certain predictions. While the machine learning models that power self-driving cars are black boxes, machine learning models in healthcare need to be open books.

And that means building different kinds of deep learning systems. To recognise the difference between, say, a canary and a hawk, a machine learning system has to work out where the boundary is between the two types of bird. To do this it needs lots of data. The more data you add, the more complex this boundary gets, and the better the machine learning system becomes at differentiating between a canary and a hawk. This is similar to the way humans memorise things – we take large amounts of data and we simplify the output, with the boundary of how we create that memory forming something of a black box. That's great for computer vision, but terrible when you need to make a specific prediction about a patient's likelihood of developing a certain disease, based on a deep analysis of their health data.

To tackle this problem, Gerstein has developed a deep learning model that's biological as well as computational. It's best thought of as being constructed from a number of different layers. At the top are the phenotypes, or traits, of a disease such as schizophrenia. At the bottom are the genetic variations that could potentially cause the disease. The neural network is trying to predict how you get from cause to effect – from genetic variations to the likelihood of having a certain disease. And to do that, Gerstein has embedded the actual gene regulatory network into the middle of the machine. This means that when it makes a prediction, Gerstein can see which pathways are turned on in the network, based on the actual genes, regulatory connections and regulatory elements found in the physical world.

'It's hard-coded into the model, which is why the model is more interpretable,' he says. 'This is very different from what people normally do.' In a traditional machine learning predictor, what goes on in the middle is mostly a mystery. In Gerstein's, that mystery has been turned into a biological network. It's a computer made up of a tiny little bit of human. 'This has the actual network – and that network has an important structure.' As it makes its predictions, the pathways burst into life, bringing light where once there was only darkness. 'Science,' says Gerstein, 'is not satisfied with a black box.'

CHAPTER SIX

The end of ageing?

The Kahn siblings knew how to live. Leonore died in 2005 at the age of 101. Helen was 109 when she passed away in 2011. In 2013 Peter died at the age of 103. Finally, Irving died in 2015 at the age of 109. Collectively, they are the world's oldest living quartet of siblings. When they were born, average life expectancy at birth was 40 years. For many centenarians the usual rules for a long, healthy life don't apply. Helen smoked all day, every day, for more than 90 years. Why didn't she stop? Simple. All four of the doctors who told her to do so died before she did. Helen also hated eating salads and vegetables, but loved chocolates, cocktails and keeping irregular hours. Irving was the oldest active investor on Wall Street and continued working at the asset-management firm that he founded until the age of 108. Irving's son, Thomas, once said his father's lifelong diet was 'lamb chops one night, steak the next'.

Humans aren't built to last for ever, but the Kahn siblings were living proof that some of us are built to last a lot longer than others. The Kahns are also part of a landmark study to uncover the secrets of living healthier for longer. The study, which started in 1998 and continues to this day, is led by Nir Barzilai, director of the Institute for Aging Research at the Albert Einstein College of Medicine in New York. 'We're discovering longevity genes,' says Barzilai. His ultimate aim is to target and delay the onset of disease, helping us live well into retirement without losing our independence.

To do this, Barzilai and his colleagues have spent decades studying a cohort of Ashkenazi Jews living in New York. This community isn't predisposed to longevity, but, as a result of persecution, intermarriage and other factors, it is remarkably genetically homo-geneous. According to markers in the DNA of their mitochondria, 40 per cent of all Ashkenazi alive today are descended from just four mothers. This lack of diversity makes spotting genetic variations linked to disease – or, in this case, longevity – comparatively easy. Most members of the Ashkenazi community in New York also have a fairly similar economic status, which helps to level out other variables that can confuse studies of longevity. To date, Barzilai and his colleagues have studied more than 500 Ashkenazi centenarians and 700 of their offspring, to track down the biomarkers of an unusually long, healthy life.

One of the key findings, as suggested by Helen's love of smoking, is that centenarians don't have healthier lifestyles than the rest of us. They don't forgo alcohol and live on a diet of oily fish and strict exercise routines. Nearly 50 per cent of the centenarians in Barzilai's study were overweight, around 50 per cent smoked and fewer than 50 per cent did even moderate exercise. Just 2 per cent were vegetarians. That doesn't mean you should ditch a healthy lifestyle and develop a penchant for cigars, but it does mean that other factors, currently beyond our control, play an important role in determining the limit of how long we can live. While a good diet and a healthy lifestyle will give you a better chance of making it to 80 in good health, it is your genes that will determine whether or not you make it past 100.

We've known for some time that our genes have a huge influence on how long we are likely to live. Twin studies have consistently shown that in cohorts born around 100 years ago, approximately 25 per cent of the variation in lifespan is a result of genetic variation. And so, armed with data, Barzilai and his colleagues set out to track down those variations. His research has uncovered a range of biomarkers that may help to explain exceptional longevity. These biomarkers are linked to clusters of genetic variations. Not all centenarians have all of the variations, but clear patterns have emerged. Around 18 per cent of the centenarians in Barzilai's cohort have a variant in a gene known as CETP, which gives them high levels of high-density lipoprotein, a type of cholesterol that protects against heart attacks and dementia. A variation of the APOC3 gene, found in about 20 per cent of the centenarians in the study, resulted in higher levels of good cholesterol and lower levels of fatty triglycerides, which are often found in high levels in people who are obese. Close to 60 per cent of the centenarians have a defect in the growth-hormone signalling pathway that helps the body switch from using energy to grow to using energy to survive – a useful strategy if you plan on being around to celebrate your 100th birthday in style. Other clusters of centenarians have unusually high levels of proteins that originate in the mitochondria and help protect against the stresses of ageing. The research has created a pharmaceutical hit list. We now know some of the biomarkers of longevity. The question is: can we develop drugs that unlock their powers?

Targeting ageing like we target disease makes a whole lot of sense. The most common risk factor for serious disease is, after all, old age. Take heart disease, for example. 'You might say cholesterol,' says Barzilai. 'No, cholesterol is a threefold risk. Ageing is a thousandfold risk.' For diabetes, obesity is an eightfold risk, but ageing is a 500-fold risk. It's the same for cancer, diabetes, neurological conditions – you name it, ageing is the most common risk factor. The problem with getting old is that, for many of us, it means numerous years of accumulating different diseases. Say you get your first serious disease at the age of 60, this is soon followed by a second and a third. At this point your body can't cope and you die before you turn 80.

That's not the case for centenarians. Studies have shown that, at the age of 100, around 23 per cent of centenarians have no chronic diseases, and 55 per cent reach 100 without cognitive impairment. This doesn't mean centenarians don't get diseases; it just means they get them at a much older age. Most people live with debilitating diseases for many years before they die. Centenarians often only get ill months, or even weeks, before they die. 'You don't have to spend eight years at the end of your life sick and begging for death,' says Barzilai. This idea is known as 'compression of morbidity'

– you live a long, healthy life and then you die. Barzilai believes that tackling this issue could save the global economy many trillions of dollars in medical and other associated costs of caring for an ageing population. 'The only way to make a difference is to actually target ageing and not target disease,' he says.

The aim here isn't to unlock immortality. By one calculation, the upper limit of the human lifespan is 115 years. Today the average life expectancy is around 80 years. Somewhere, somehow, the majority of us are missing out on 35 years of our lives. In the coming years Barzilai hopes to start gaining back some of those lost years. But while we have a plethora of drugs that target and treat serious diseases, we don't have a single drug we can prescribe that targets ageing. That's because ageing – unlike, say, prostate cancer – doesn't have one specific, universal biomarker. But as we come to understand more about what ageing actually is, we're getting closer to understanding how we might slow it down.

Chances are you, or someone you know, takes metformin. This unremarkable little pill is used to treat Type 2 diabetes and is the fourth-most commonly prescribed medication in the United States, with some 78 million annual prescriptions in 2017 alone. Metformin has been around since 1957, but its history goes back to the Middle Ages when French lilac, the plant from which it is derived, was prescribed as a treatment for frequent urination – something that we now know to be a sign of diabetes. Metformin has quietly earned itself the unlikely reputation as a potential wonder-drug. Compared to people with diabetes taking other drugs, people with diabetes taking metformin live longer, have fewer cardiovascular issues and, bizarrely, appear to get cancer 10 per cent less often. Besides its intended effect on blood glucose, metformin also has an impact on pathways involved in growth, inflammation and metabolism – all of which have an effect on ageing. Metformin also inhibits oxygen consumption in mitochondria, effectively easing the amount of work done by the tiny powerhouses that fuel our cells. Six of the centenarians in Barzilai's study had a genetic mutation that delivered a similar benefit – their mitochondria worked less intensely and took longer to degrade.

Barzilai is now working on a study that will investigate whether metformin could be prescribed as the first ever drug to target ageing. The study, known as Targeting Aging with Metformin, or TAME, will run for six years across 14 research institutions in the US and will gather data from 3,000 people between the ages of 65 and 79. It will aim to answer a crucial question: do people who take metformin stay healthier for longer? Other drugs, some of which are already available, might do a better job, but few are as safe, cheap and widely used as metformin. Rapamycin, for example, outperformed metformin in longevity studies on animals, but the immunosuppressant has potentially dangerous side-effects. Metformin doesn't. And that's key for one reason: with many of the technical hurdles cleared, one of the key barriers to treating ageing as a disease is regulatory approval. If the metformin trial is a success, Barzilai is hopeful that the FDA and other regulators will finally recognise ageing as a condition worthy of targeting. This decision, if and when it comes, will likely create a pharmaceutical and biotechnology gold rush.

But in the race for longevity, some people are not so patient. Or so realistic. Several biotechnology companies, fuelled by Silicon Valley fortunes, are out to solve death. Peter Thiel, the billionaire founder of PayPal, and Amazon's Jeff Bezos are among those to have championed or heavily invested in the longevity cause. Aubrey de Grey, an author and academic who is on a self-professed 'crusade to defeat ageing', proposes that the first human beings who will live to 1,000 years old have already been born. The fantastical notion that we might be able to live for many hundreds of years is the subject of TED Talks (de Grey's alone has more than four million views on YouTube) and the focus of Google's multibillion-dollar Calico 'longevity' lab. Bill Maris, the entrepreneur and venture capitalist who founded Calico, has said that people could live 'for 500 years'. Since 2016 Ambrosia, a start-up based in California, has been selling 'young blood transfusions' – the blood of children, transfused into the bodies of adults – for $8,000 a litre, despite little to no evidence that such a procedure has any health benefits. Unity Biotechnology, also based in California, is working to 'prevent, halt and reverse various diseases of ageing'. To date it has raised more than $210 million in funding. Ray Kurzweil, a director of engineering at Google, posits that there is a longevity 'escape velocity' – the point at which scientific advances add years to our lives more quickly than they pass. That point, he believes, is less than a decade away.

But why wait? On 15 September 2015, Elizabeth Parrish, the 44-year-old founder of biotechnology firm BioViva, walked into a clinic in Bogotá, Colombia. Over several hours she received more than 100 injections all over her body. Those injections contained two largely untested and potentially harmful gene therapies, both of which aimed to treat the same disease: ageing. Parrish, in a shroud of secrecy, had become a human guinea pig in an outlandish experiment. The gene therapy she received, conducted in South America to skirt federal regulations in the US, had been tested on animals but remained many years – potentially decades – from being approved and safe for use in humans. One of these gene therapies was a myostatin inhibitor, a drug to reverse muscle loss. The other was a telomerase gene therapy, which encourages cells to produce telomerase, a protein that repairs telomeres. The experiment made headlines around the world and turned Parrish into an overnight celebrity. Experts criticised the experiment for being unethical, poorly conceived and potentially dangerous.

But, Parrish claims, it worked. Telomeres sit at the tips of chromosomes and act as guardians, protecting important genetic material from damage. But as cells divide and DNA replicates, telomeres become shorter and shorter. Eventually they become so short that cells can divide no more. While scientists have found correlations between health and telomere length, it remains unclear if shorter telomeres cause health problems or are simply a side-effect of ageing. Parrish claims that, six months after her treatment in Bogotá, third-party testing showed the telomeres in her white blood cells had lengthened by 9 per cent. If true, that would mean the procedure reversed 20 years of normal telomere shortening. But caveats abound. Lengthening telomeres in this way could be the equivalent of dyeing grey hair brown again – you're still the same age, it just doesn't look like it. And the final catch: most labs that measure telomere length have an 8 per cent margin of error.

Such bumps in the road have done little to slow the progress of an industry powered by an almost religious zeal to uncover the fountain of youth. 'We're looking at a variety of different candidates to cure ageing,' says Parrish. Since her treatment in Colombia, BioViva has morphed into what she describes as a 'data analysis company' and has partnered with Integrated Health Systems, a gene-therapy company, to hook up people and companies interested in experimental gene therapies that target ageing with doctors who are willing to carry them out. 'We go between Mexico, the Dominican Republic, Peru, Colombia,' Parrish says, listing the countries in which patients are able to receive gene therapies that are banned in most of the world. In 2016 BioViva, in partnership with Sierra Sciences – another biotech company founded by Bill Andrews, the molecular biologist who made part of Parrish's gene therapy – announced plans to open an anti-ageing clinic in Fiji. At the time Andrews said the clinic would be 'done' by the end of the year. No such clinic has ever been built. Andrews has since gone on to found Libella Gene Therapeutics, based in Kansas, which claims to offer gene therapy to repair telomeres at a clinic in Colombia for $1 million a dose, as part of a so-called pay-to-play 'clinical trial'. With patient numbers low, costs high and the associated risks even higher, Parrish is now pinning her hopes on what little data there is to glean from this Wild West industry. 'We have a lot of companies interested in seeing if their drugs work,' she claims. BioViva's pivot to data analysis, she claims, puts it front and centre. The company hopes to act as a data aggregation and analysis platform, bringing together results from the controversial gene-therapy treatments administered in Central and South America. 'Hopefully we'll be able to bring ten, twenty, thirty patients' data to investors and let them see where the impact of the drugs were in a multitude of people,' she says. 'We're hoping that investors will come up fast to run those drugs through regulation because they know they'll be onto a winner.'

She might be genetically modified, but Parrish is not a medical doctor. When she announced to the world that she had conducted gene therapy on herself, one of BioViva's most senior scientific advisers, George Martin, a professor at the University of Washington, immediately resigned, saying he was 'very upset' by what had happened. 'I would urge lots of preclinical studies,' he said at the time. As the scientific community turns its back on an industry seemingly hell-bent on skirting regulations and academic rigour, Parrish is taking another route. In January 2020 she gave an hour-long talk at the Church of Perpetual Life. 'I'm the CEO of BioViva,' she said. 'And I do want to genetically engineer you,' she told the congregation. The church, which was founded in 2013 and is based in Hollywood, Florida, is attended by immortalists and transhumanists and has a simple motto: 'ageing and death can be optional'. One of its prophets is the science-fiction writer Arthur C. Clarke. Its founder, William Faloon, once claimed the FDA was part of 'a conspiracy to commit genocide against the American people'. For an industry that's trying to persuade the world that the science is ready but the regulation is not, such associations create a bad look. But Parrish is adamant it is the system, not the science, that is broken. 'We're not going to slow down for a system that has held back this technology for decades. Our risk aversion is killing us,' she says.

The science of targeting ageing as a disease is one being buffeted by religion, impatience and hubris. From the company charging people thousands of dollars to be infused with the blood of children, to the Silicon Valley investor suggesting we may soon live to the age of 500, it is at risk of being overrun by ego. But it needn't be. 'I think there is a perception that living a long and healthy life is only for the rich people,' says Barzilai. 'This is the wrong way to look at it. It's a real issue and it worries me.' Genetic therapies that target ageing may, in time, be shown to work and become more mainstream. But such advancements will bring with them a cavalcade of confounding ethical questions. Using gene therapies to ensure good health could have great benefits. But what about using gene therapies to make people more athletic or intelligent? Our society, let alone our regulators and lawmakers, are nowhere near ready to tackle such questions. But as Barzilai's centenarians have shown, the secrets of a long, healthy life already lurk within our own bodies.

In unlocking that potential, we will all benefit from the bravery and commitment of the pioneers of the present – the patients and doctors putting their lives and careers on the line so that we might all one day benefit.

We will celebrate our later years in good health, thankful for the extra time we have to enjoy with our children, grandchildren and great-grandchildren. The societal and economic benefits will be profound. Perhaps we will raise a glass to the omics data and personalised medicine that has enabled us to stay so healthy for so long. But, most likely, we won't. Instead we will diligently take the pills we have been prescribed to replicate the mutations and variations of longevity, affording ourselves an extra decade or two of good health. After all, nobody really wants to live for ever – they just want to live better.

Index